RELIGION AT THE POLLS

RELIGION
AT THE POLLS

by
Albert J. Menendez

THE WESTMINSTER PRESS

PHILADELPHIA

Book Design by Dorothy Alden Smith

Published by The Westminster Press ®
Philadelphia, Pennsylvania

PRINTED IN THE UNITED STATES OF AMERICA

Library of Congress Cataloging in Publication Data

Menendez, Albert J
  Religion at the polls.

  Bibliography: p.
  1. Religion and politics—United States. 2. Presidents
—United States—Election—History. I. Title.
BL2530.U6M46   261.7'0973   76–30655
ISBN 0–664–24117–4

HC 2127

To Shirley

Contents

Introduction:
Why Religious Groups Vote as They Do

Like George Bernard Shaw, I have always believed that religion and politics, the proverbial no-no's of polite conversation, are the only truly interesting and endlessly absorbing subjects. They reach a particularly high level of fascination when they commingle and interact. It is the entanglement between religion and politics that forms the basis of this investigation.

What I have attempted in this book is to look at the specific historical instances in which religion affected the tone, debate, and outcome of Presidential elections. The way in which religion shaped the cultural milieu is also considered. The influence of religion on Congressional decisions and referendum elections in recent years is given some discussion.

Neither have I neglected the present rebirth of religion in politics. Speaking in Pennsylvania during the state's pivotal primary, on April 23, 1976, Senator Henry M. Jackson of Washington made a remarkable statement: "When a fellow starts telling how religious he is, I sort of become suspicious. I've taught Sunday school, but I'm not making my relationship with the Lord an issue in the campaign." What was Jackson talking about? Had a religious issue suddenly resurfaced into the American political mainstream?

Undoubtedly Jackson was referring to the prominently

expressed religious convictions of Democratic front-run-
ner, former Georgia Governor Jimmy Carter. For the
first time since 1960, religious views suddenly became a
political issue. No one suggested that Carter's Baptist
church would improperly influence his decisions.
Rather, some critics have suggested that Carter's deep
personal commitment to evangelical Protestant Christianity might somehow be a liability in our religiously pluralistic society. There was nothing in Carter's public record to substantiate such fears, but a number of colum-
nists, theologians, and journalists did raise the question.

As I see it, there are only four ways in which a candidate's religion could raise doubts about his fitness to
hold office. If a candidate were: (1) to have a messianic
complex, in which he regarded his every decision as the
will of God; (2) to discriminate in favor of or against
certain religions in his policies or appointments; (3) to
use his position to enhance or promote sectarian values;
or (4) to combine the civil and religious roles in his
Presidential office. Given the nature of our democracy,
it is unlikely that anyone that insensitive to America's
religious pluralism could be nominated by either of our
two major parties. Even if these conditions were to exist,
the Constitutional prohibition (Article VI) against religious tests for public office would still be valid.

Nevertheless, the concern expressed by so many per-
sons about the political implications of a man's obviously
sincere religious faith indicates the need for a fresh, new
look at religion's impact on the political process
throughout American history. We shall try to answer
such basic questions as these:

1. Do individuals tend to vote for their coreligionists?
2. Are members of certain religious groups intrinsically conservative or liberal politically, and if so, why?
3. Do adherents of certain religions tend to vote a

certain way when they are members of Congress?

4. Do the distinctive tenets of our many religious traditions produce a particular frame of reference within which believers make their political decisions?

5. Is there still substantial prejudice against electing members of certain faiths to public office?

6. Are there present church-state issues that will likely affect the outcome of elections?

7. Does the resurgence of evangelicalism in politics presage a new era of political conflict on religious lines?

8. To what extent does religion interact with other variables, such as social status, geographical location, and ethnicity?

9. Will religion ever again determine the outcome of an American Presidential election?

10. Will the evangelicals vote as a bloc to support one of their own for President?

Through the course of this book we shall attempt to find some reasonable answers, based on empirical evidence, to these and other questions.

I have sought to approach this controversial subject with the objectivity and detachment required by my profession, but I cannot confess to complete impartiality. I have my biases and opinions, though I trust they are not pervasive. I loathe religious prejudice and bigotry and oppose attempts to divide the electorate along religious lines. I subscribe fully to the U.S. Supreme Court's warning: "Political division along religious lines was one of the principal evils against which the First Amendment was intended to protect"(*Lemon* v. *Kurtzman* and *Early* v. *Dicenso,* 1971). I cherish our highly developed religious liberty and feel utter contempt for those who have sought to deny the Presidency to any religious group.

I have extensively reviewed the literature in the field and have ferreted out relevant material that has been written on the relationship of religion to politics. I have summarized the primary findings of scholars and specialists who have researched various phases of the general subject. Previously most of this information has not been available in one place.

In addition, I have used available published resources to determine the predominant religious affiliation of each county in the United States. This information is derived from *Churches and Church Membership in the United States, 1971,* by Douglas W. Johnson, Paul R. Picard, and Bernard Quinn. For background comparison, I also consulted the 1926 *U.S. Census of Religious Bodies.* Counties and political subdivisions can then be classified according to the predominant religious pattern. Evangelical counties, for example, are generally those which have a large membership in leading evangelical Protestant churches and a correspondingly low Catholic population. The voting behavior over several elections can then be traced. I have not attempted to verify the data by sophisticated statistical techniques, such as regression analysis, because this is a book for the general reader and I am concerned with the general patterns of voting among large religious groups.

Statistics presented in Tables 1, 2, 3, 4, 5, and 13, in the Appendix are based on information contained in *Religion in America 1976,* Gallup Opinion Index, Report No. 130. Table 14 is from *Church & State,* April 1974.

I have also used extensive public opinion data from several prominent opinion polling organizations. On occasion I refer to a survey I personally conducted in 1974. This survey was predicated on standard sampling design methods and other research techniques utilized by public opinion surveys, with which I have some familiarity. This survey dealt with a small sample of the population and is introduced only in dealing with a couple of subgroups. I have not included all my statistical findings in this book, because the general reader will probably not be interested in the enormous number of charts and tables which show the data in minute detail. Some of the more important aspects of the data have been retained.

I am indebted to four individuals whom I interviewed in person or by mail: the two prominent specialists on religion in politics, Dr. Seymour Martin Lipset, fellow of the Hoover Institution on War, Peace and Revolution at Stanford University, and Dr. Lawrence H. Fuchs, chairman of the American Studies Department at Brandeis University; Richard M. Scammon, America's foremost authority on elections and director of the Elections Research Center in Washington, D.C.; and Dr. Harold O. J. Brown, evangelical scholar, author, and seminary instructor. I am also appreciative of the assistance rendered by Alice McGillivray and Linda Sutherland of the Elections Research Center.

I appreciate the typing contribution made by my fine secretary, Ms. Sharon Carey. Special appreciation goes, as always, to my wife, Shirley, for her encouragement and support.

A. J. M.

Olney, Maryland

1

America's Religious Groups:
Their Geography and Demography

Where people live, what they do for a living, and how much education they have attained are significant factors in the way they vote. Even though our main concern is religious voting, we must take account of those nonreligious elements which affect the electoral behavior of all people, irrespective of their religion. The fact that most Baptists live in the South, that most Catholics and Jews are urban dwellers, and that a considerable number of Lutherans are farmers plays a significant role in shaping and modifying the voting behavior of these groups.

GEOGRAPHY

Religiously speaking, the American states fall into several categories. The first are the *homogeneous* states in which one church is dominant. At the present time, in 22 of the 50 states one religious tradition comprises more than 50% of the total church members. It is important to note the distinction between church members and percentage of total population. In only a few states does one church comprise a majority of the entire population.

Fifteen states (Connecticut, Maine, Massachusetts, New Hampshire, Rhode Island, Vermont, New Jersey, New York, Pennsylvania, Illinois, Michigan, Louisiana, New Mexico, California, and Hawaii) are predominantly

Roman Catholic. Five states (Georgia, South Carolina, Alabama, Mississippi, and Tennessee) are predominantly Baptist, while Utah and Idaho are heavily Mormon.

Twenty-five states are *bifurcated,* i.e., two religious groups comprise over half of the church population. In Missouri, Florida, Kentucky, Texas, and Alaska, Catholics and Baptists dominate. In Ohio, Kansas, Delaware, Maryland, and Colorado, Catholics and Methodists lead. In eight Western states (Wisconsin, Iowa, Minnesota, Nebraska, Montana, Washington, North Dakota, and South Dakota) Catholics and Lutherans are strongest. In two states, Arizona and Nevada, Catholics and Mormons dominate, while in five southern states (Virginia, North Carolina, West Virginia, Arkansas, and Oklahoma) Baptists and Methodists predominate. Indeed, in nine states of the Old Confederacy and three border states, Baptists and Methodists are the overwhelming leaders.

A third category, which includes only three states, might be called *pluralistic.* These are states where it takes three or more churches to form a majority of the church membership. The most pluralistic state is Oregon, where four churches combine to make up about half of the population. The other two states are Wyoming, where 47% of the church members are either Catholic or Mormon, and Indiana, where 49% are either Catholic or Methodist.

Despite America's remarkable religious diversity, it is significant that most states tend to be dominated by one or two church traditions. We shall now briefly look at each major religious group to see where it is strongest.

Roman Catholics

America's largest church, which now claims over 48 million members and counts all baptized children as members, is strongest in New England and the large urban areas. Over half of the Roman Catholics live in just six states: New York, California, Pennsylvania, Illinois, Massachusetts, and New Jersey. If we add Ohio, Michigan, Texas, and Wisconsin, we will know where 70% of the Catholics live. Nine of the ten largest states are Catholic strongholds. Florida is the only megastate missing, while Wisconsin is the only relatively small state included in the Catholic top ten. Connecticut and Louisiana rank eleventh and twelfth in terms of total Catholic population. In only one state, Rhode Island, are Catholics a majority of the total population.

Baptists

There are almost 29 million Baptists in over twenty different associations in the United States. There are at least 12 million black Baptists, and the members of the Southern Baptist Convention number 12.7 million. There are more than 2 million Southern Baptists in Texas, and over 1 million in Georgia, North Carolina, and Tennessee. Other strongholds include Kentucky, Florida, Alabama, South Carolina, Mississippi, and Oklahoma. There are about 1.5 million American Baptists, who are historically strong in Indiana, West Virginia, Ohio, and Illinois. Their membership also exceeds 100,000 in California, New York, and Pennsylvania.

Methodists

The 11.5 million Methodists (mostly in The United Methodist Church) are scattered widely throughout the country, though about half live in eleven states. They are most numerous in Texas and Ohio. Other large Methodist populations are found in Pennsylvania, Illinois, North Carolina, New York, Virginia, Indiana, Georgia,

Tennessee, Florida, and Iowa. They are the largest single church only in West Virginia.

Lutherans

America's nearly 9 million Lutherans are heavily concentrated in the Midwest and in Pennsylvania. Over one third of America's Lutherans live in just three states: Minnesota, Wisconsin, and Pennsylvania. The next strongest Lutheran states are Illinois, Ohio, New York, Iowa, and California. They are the largest denomination in Minnesota, North Dakota, and South Dakota.

Jews

About 40% of America's 6 million Jews live in New York, where they constitute one out of seven residents. California, Pennsylvania, New Jersey, Illinois, Massachusetts, Florida, and Maryland have substantial Jewish constituencies.

Presbyterians

America's 4 million Presbyterians are widely dispersed, though their historic stronghold is Pennsylvania. At one time almost one fourth of America's Presbyterians lived in Pennsylvania, though today about 12% do. There are also large numbers of Presbyterians in New York, California, Ohio, New Jersey, North Carolina, Texas, and Michigan.

Episcopalians

The 3 million Episcopalians are primarily found in the Eastern Seaboard states from Florida to Maine. They are still quite strong in many of the coastal counties, and they are relatively strong in New York City, Philadelphia, Boston, and Washington. Among the smaller states they are strong in Delaware, Wyoming, and Rhode Island. There are more than 100,000 Episcopalians in New York, California, Pennsylvania, Texas, New Jersey, Massachusetts, Florida, Virginia, Connecticut, Michigan, and Maryland.

United Church of Christ

This 2-million-member religious body is strongest in New England, the Midwest, and Pennsylvania. It has over 100,000 members in Pennsylvania, Ohio, and Illinois, where most were formerly associated with the Evangelical and Reformed Church, and in Massachusetts and Connecticut, where most were at one time Congregationalists. In Wisconsin the 105,000 UCC members came from both of the previous traditions.

Mormons

This fast-growing religious group, which has increased its membership from 2.1 to 2.7 million in the last four years, is found mostly in the Far West. Over half of its members are located in Utah and California, with other large representations in Idaho and Arizona. Mormons comprise 89% of the church members in Utah and 51% in Idaho. They also constitute 26% of the church members in Nevada, 18% in Wyoming, and 13% in Arizona.

A Final Word on Geography

Americans are a highly mobile people. The average American moves frequently and has lived in several parts of the country. The newest Gallup data show that a con-

siderable number of Jews and Catholics have moved
from the East to the South in the last decade. A slightly
lower percentage of Methodists have moved in the opposite direction. (Methodists and Presbyterians are more
evenly distributed throughout the nation than other
groups.) Though a majority of Jews still live in the East,
Baptists in the South, and Lutherans in the Midwest,
there is geographical movement that may affect future
elections. (See Appendix, Table 1.)

Similarly, there was a shift in the last half decade from
large cities to rural and small-town areas, often in the
exurbs or suburbs of large metropolitan centers. Among
Jews and Catholics especially has there been a move out
of the cities. Only 54% of the Jews, compared to 66% in
1971, now live in cities of over one million population,
while 12% now live in rural–small-town areas. More
Catholics (30%) now live in small towns than in large
cities (25%). A smaller trend among Episcopalians (4%)
toward rural–small-town living turns up in Gallup's *Religion in America 1976.* On the other hand, fewer Baptists,
Methodists, and Lutherans live in rural America. They
have moved (at least 2% to 3% of them) into larger
cities. These changes in the location and distribution of
religious groups are surely matters of political significance. (See Appendix, Table 2.)

DEMOGRAPHY

Throughout most of America's history, the high-status
religious groups have tended to be Anglo-Saxon in background and Eastern in geography, e.g., Episcopalians,
Congregationalists, and Presbyterians. Jews began as
poor immigrants but rapidly prospered through education and industry, becoming one of the true success stories of the American dream. Methodists and Lutherans
tended toward the middle of the spectrum, while Roman

Catholics and Baptists were predominantly working class. This basic pattern has continued, though the socioeconomic gap between religions has lessened considerably since World War II.

The first postwar analysis of socioeconomic status was made by the Office of Public Opinion Research at Princeton University in 1945 and 1946. It showed Episcopalians, Christian Scientists, Congregationalists, Presbyterians, and Jews at the top of the social spectrum, followed closely by the Reformed churches. In the middle were Methodists and Lutherans, while Catholics, Baptists, and Mormons were primarily lower middle class. Twenty-four percent of the Episcopalians, for example, were "upper class," compared to 8% of the Baptists.[1]

Bernard Lazerwitz, writing in 1961 but using 1956–57 data, found substantially identical patterns, though Episcopalians and Jews had moved far ahead of the pack and Baptists had slipped farther into last place. Roman Catholics surged ahead somewhat, passing Lutherans and Methodists.[2]

A 1957 special U.S. Government census of religious bodies found the same general ranking and added some new information about occupations. Episcopalians, Jews, and Presbyterians were found to be primarily engaged in professional, managerial, and clerical professions, while Catholics and Baptists were more likely to be skilled or unskilled laborers. Lutherans and Methodists leaned somewhat toward the laboring column. Fifteen percent of the Lutherans and 11% of the Baptists were farmers. A substantially similar result was revealed by a 1971 Gallup survey, though a higher percentage of all religions were engaged in professional, clerical, and sales occupations. The income distributions within groups followed the historic patterns. Most Episcopalians, Jews, and Presbyterians were upper and middle class. The other groups were preponderantly middle to lower middle class. This does not mean, of course, that there are no rich Baptists nor poor Jews, because there are. There has been a rather dramatic improvement in the social and economic status of most Americans in the last quarter century. (See Appendix, Tables 3 and 4.)

The irrepressible Andrew M. Greeley offered a mild dissent in late 1975. Using a composite sample of twelve National Opinion Research Center surveys, Greeley claimed that, in income at least, Roman Catholics had moved into second place, behind Jews. However, his survey excluded the Spanish-speaking and blacks, which might tend to skew the data. Greeley found that Irish, Italian, German, and Polish Catholics ranked just behind Jews in income. Episcopalians, Presbyterians, Slavic Catholics, British Protestants, French Catholics, Methodists, and Lutherans were next. German, Scandinavian, "American," and Irish Protestants followed, with Baptists placing last. Income, however, is only one phase of social status. Greeley's own summary concluded: "Jews, Episcopalians, and Presbyterians are not only the most successful of Americans in terms of occupational stratification; they are also the most successful in terms of occupational mobility, holding constant their own and parental education. Baptists and Lutherans are substantially less successful both in stratification and mobility and Catholics and Methodists hover close to the average."[3] Greeley's income findings are challenged by Thomas Sowell[4] and Andrew Hacker.[5]

To an extent, educational attainment is a correlate of social prominence and a major determinant of voting behavior. The same religious groups at the top of the occupational scale dominate the educational achievement scale. The 1957 U.S. Census showed that 28% of the Episcopalians were college graduates, followed by 16% of the Jews and the Presbyterians, 11% of the Methodists, 5% of the Lutherans and the Catholics, and 4%

of the Baptists. By 1971, 47% of the Episcopalians, 42% of the Jews, and 39% of the Presbyterians had attended college. So had 24% of the Methodists, 22% of the Lutherans, 21% of the Catholics, and 12% of the Baptists. The latest data for 1975 show about the same picture, though Jews have now achieved parity with Episcopalians for first place. (See Appendix, Table 5.)

One final piece of fascinating data is contained in a study of the religious preferences of the university professoriate by Seymour Martin Lipset and Everett Ladd. They found that almost half of the college professors were Jews, Episcopalians, Presbyterians, or members of the United Church of Christ. The more prestigious the college, the higher the percentage of faculty belonging to these high-status groups. Roman Catholics are slightly underrepresented but have improved their showing considerably since the last sampling, especially among younger professors. Baptists, Methodists, and Lutherans are consistently underrepresented.[6]

2

Religion and the Presidency, 1789–1928

Religion, even in a nation that constitutionally separates church and state, cannot be totally divorced from politics. Many public issues have religious or ethical dimensions, and the religious sentiments of individual candidates have often become campaign issues. As Dulce and Richter maintained, religion has "figured prominently in an average of one of every three campaigns for the Presidency through 1960."[1]

Thomas Jefferson, the great patriot and tireless exponent of religious liberty, was the first candidate to face the brunt of religious smears. Though born an Anglican, Jefferson adopted liberal deistic views and was more concerned with the ethical rather than the dogmatic aspects of religion. His opposition to religious establishment and discrimination against non-Anglicans in Virginia did not endear him to Anglican voters. He was very popular among Presbyterians and Baptists, the main religious groups to benefit from the disestablishment of Anglicanism and the passage of his Act for Establishing Religious Freedom in Virginia on December 5, 1785.

It would be fascinating in retrospect to see how his Presbyterian admirers, who became the bulwark of the Democratic Party in Pennsylvania, would have responded if the following letter had been made public during his lifetime:

The Presbyterian clergy are the loudest, the most intolerant of all sects; the most tyrannical and ambitious, ready at the word of the law-giver, if such a word could now be obtained, to put their torch to the pile, and to rekindle in this virgin hemisphere the flame in which their oracle, Calvin, consumed the poor Servetus, because he could not subscribe to the proposition of Calvin, that magistrates have a right to exterminate all heretics to the Calvinistic creed! They pant to re-establish by law that holy inquisition which they can now only infuse into public opinion.[2]

Jefferson's outspoken free thought became an issue in the 1800 election. Violent attacks from the Puritan pulpit in New England were commonplace. One preacher warned his listeners that they would have to hide their Bibles in their wells if Jefferson were elected.[3] He was variously called a spendthrift, a libertine, and an atheist. Federalist pamphleteer J. M. Mason published *Serious Considerations on the Election of a President, and a Voice of Warning to Christians in the Ensuing Election,* in which he warned that "religion will be destroyed and immorality would flourish" if the "infidel" Jefferson became President.[4] Obviously, most electors disagreed, because Jefferson won, albeit narrowly, the election.

Jefferson continued the same strong church-state separationist views while President, refusing to proclaim a Day of Thanksgiving, but he was easily reelected in 1804. The fact that only a small number of Americans were church members may have contributed to his popularity.

During Andrew Jackson's first campaign for the Presidency in 1824, an emotional whispering campaign alleging that he and his wife, Rachel, were not validly married surfaced in many states. The blatant dishonesty of the attacks hurt and embittered Jackson, who blamed his critics for the premature death of Rachel, shortly after his 1828 victory.

Organized anti-Catholicism erupted in the 1830's and 1840's, stimulated by the influx of Irish Catholics and the fear of popish invasion by militant Protestants. Journalist Samuel F. B. Morse, in a series of pseudonymous newspaper articles and a book *A Foreign Conspiracy Against the Liberties of the United States,* promoted the view that the Catholic countries of the Holy Alliance and the papacy were conspiring to subvert Protestant America. Religious extremism characterized this period, culminating in the burning of a Charlestown, Massachusetts, convent by a Protestant mob, and church burnings in Philadelphia in 1844. A flood of anti-Catholic literature and organizations is vividly described by historian Ray Allen Billington in his excellent book *The Protestant Crusade, 1800–1860.* Bills were introduced in several state legislatures to restrict voting rights to native-born Protestants.

The 1844 election was extremely close, with Democrat James K. Polk handing Whig Henry Clay his third Presidential defeat. Though no sophisticated election analysis was possible, Whigs, including future President Millard Fillmore, blamed "foreign Catholics" for their defeat, a refrain that would be heard again and again for the next century and more by the enemies of the Democratic Party.

In the 1850's a group of extremists constituted themselves as the "know-nothing" or Native American Party. They loathed Roman Catholics and foreigners and were convinced that American institutions were Protestant to the core and would be jeopardized if Catholics were to hold public office.

In the 1852 campaign the Democrat, Franklin Pierce, of New Hampshire, was criticized by many Catholics because his state still maintained a test act against Catholic officeholders. The voters of the strongly anti-Catholic state had declined to remove the requirement. The Whig candidate, General Winfield Scott, was accused of having hanged Irish Catholic deserters during the Mexican War. Both candidates were accused of having daughters who became nuns. Pierce won by a landslide and promptly appointed a Catholic, James Campbell of Pennsylvania, Postmaster General.

The Know-Nothings (Nativists) gained strength and were responsible for the mobbing of papal emissary Bedini when he toured the United States in 1853. In 1854, amid rioting in Louisville and elsewhere, the Know-Nothings won 8 senators out of 62, 124 Congressmen out of 234, and swept local offices in Massachusetts, Delaware, Pennsylvania, Maryland, and Kentucky. Revision of immigration laws was a primary legislative goal.

In 1856 the Nativists ran former President Millard Fillmore, a Unitarian, for President. The newly formed Republican Party nominated the popular soldier-explorer John C. Frémont, who soon became the object of an absurd whispering campaign that he was a Catholic and that his daughter was educated in a convent. (He was an Episcopalian.) The Democrats nominated James Buchanan, of Pennsylvania, and adopted a platform blasting religious prejudice. Buchanan won easily, Frémont did respectably well, sweeping much of the North, and Fillmore carried only Maryland. Division among the Nativists over slavery overshadowed the religious issue. The movement vanished, only to reappear under new names and leaders in the 1890's.

The Civil War mitigated religious prejudice and the religious issue was absent from the 1860 and 1864 elections. However, as Vincent P. de Santis discovered, "Catholicism had no real significance in any one of the presidential elections of the post-Civil War generation. As an issue, and even as a propaganda device, it was always overshadowed by other matters. Whether Catholicism would have become an important factor if a Catholic had run for President we shall never know, for neither one of the major parties seriously considered a Catholic as a candidate for the presidency. From this it might appear that they were unwilling to take the risk of running a Catholic for President, and that this reluctance excluded presidential possibilities who, had they not been Catholics, might have otherwise been considered or named. But such a conclusion rests more upon emotionalism than it does upon historical evidence. No doubt there would have been sturdy obstacles in the way of running a Catholic for the presidency, but how much of a risk or liability such a nomination would have been to a party in these years will never be known. There is no evidence to warrant the conclusion that the major parties held back from naming a Catholic because of the risk element involved. More to the point is the fact that there were no Catholics prominent, popular, or attractive enough for the parties to consider. We do know, though, that Catholicism did provoke bitter political fights in local and state contests."[5]

In 1872, *Harper's Weekly,* a Republican paper, blasted the Catholic-Democratic alliance and called Horace Greeley "a noted opponent of the Bible and a firm friend of Rome." It called upon "every sincere Protestant to labor ceaselessly to defeat the schemes of the Jesuits, and drive their candidate back to a merited obscurity."[6]

In the mid-1870's the issue of public aid for sectarian schools reared its head, as it had briefly in the 1830's and '40s. President Ulysses S. Grant, speaking to Union Army veterans in Des Moines, Iowa, on September 25, 1875, said: "Encourage free schools and resolve that not one dollar appropriated for their support shall be appropriated to the support of any sectarian schools. Resolve that neither the state nor nation, nor both combined, shall support institutions of learning other than those sufficient to afford every child growing up in the land of

opportunity of a good common school education, un-
mixed with sectarian, pagan, or atheistical dogmas.
Leave the matter of religion to the family altar, the
church and the private school supported entirely by private contributions. Keep the church and state forever
separate."

Though a constitutional amendment to prohibit government aid to parochial schools narrowly failed of passage, it became a crucial political issue through the re-
mainder of the century, and the Republicans reiterated
their endorsement in party platforms through 1892.

In 1876, *Harper's Weekly* outrageously charged on July
29 that "the Vatican directs the policy of the ruling sec-
tion of the Democratic party." On October 21, the editors charged that Catholic clergy threatened to excom-
municate Catholics who voted for G.O.P. nominee
Rutherford B. Hayes, an opponent of government aid to
parochial schools.

Catholic journals rather humorously added a new twist
to the discussion. Historian John Gilmary Shea in the
American Catholic Quarterly Review (January 1876) had
written that retiring President Grant was unduly influenced by Methodist preachers. (Grant himself was a
notoriously poor churchgoer and may have been a non-
believer.)[7] Shea wrote: "That he is a Methodist is kept
constantly before the public mind. He is actually priest-
ridden. The bishops and ministers of his creed exercise
an influence that the Presbyterians never dreamed of
coveting, while Jackson or Polk were in power; or Episcopalians under Washington, Madison or Monroe."'

Hayes admired the Catholic Church's racial tolerance
and egalitarianism, though he opposed parochial school
aid. In fact he opposed "all sectarian interference with
political affairs, and especially with the schools."[8] When
early returns apparently indicated a Democratic victory,
James A. Garfield, who would succeed Hayes in 1881,

wrote privately that the Republicans had been defeated by "the combined power of rebellion, Catholicism, and whiskey."[9] The disputed election of 1876 was resolved in Hayes's favor, due to a deal with the South in which the Republicans agreed to withdraw federal troops in return for the electoral votes of South Carolina and Florida.

No religious issue surfaced in the 1880 election, though New York City elected its first Catholic mayor, William R. Grace, an anti-Tammany Hall Democrat who barely survived a hysterical religious smear campaign. He squeaked by with a 3,000-vote majority compared to a 40,000-vote spread for the Democratic Presidential candidate.[10]

In 1884 came the celebrated slogan, "Rum, Romanism, and Rebellion." The Republican nominee was James G. Blaine, "the plumed knight" (as atheist orator Robert Ingersoll called him in his nominating speech). Blaine had been U.S. Senator, Speaker of the House, and Secretary of State. Born of a Presbyterian father and an Irish Catholic mother and raised a Catholic, he had become a Presbyterian in adulthood. This, plus his anti-parochiaid amendment, was bound to alienate many Catholic voters. However, Blaine, whose cousin was mother superior of a convent, refused to countenance any criticism of his mother's faith. On the other hand, Grover Cleveland, the Democratic candidate, was not particularly popular among Catholics. The usually Democratic Catholic vote was up for grabs.

Extraneous nonsense abounded. Blaine was accused of educating one of his daughters in a convent in Paris, while allowing another daughter to be married by a "Romish priest" to a former officer of the Papal Guards.[11]

In late October a weary Blaine attended a fund-raising dinner in New York City. On the morning of October 29, at the Park Avenue Hotel, several hundred Protestant clergymen gathered to hear the candidate. They selected Rev. Samuel D. Burchard, a Presbyterian, as chairman and asked him to make a short welcoming statement. In it he said: "We expect to vote for you next Tuesday. We are Republicans and don't propose to leave our party and identify ourselves with the party whose antecedents have been rum, Romanism, and rebellion." Journalists present apparently did not hear the offensive statement or did not consider it significant. A shorthand reporter, sent by the Democratic Party, however, recorded the statement. Within days handbills were placed in Roman Catholic parishes throughout the East. Blaine called the comment "exceedingly unfortunate," but his disclaimer probably came too late.

Blaine narrowly lost New York by 1,149 votes and, thus, the election. Whether the intemperate remark of the partisan preacher played a role in the voters' decision is problematic. There were no public opinion polls and almost no viable data on which to analyze religious voting in those days. Some scholars, like historian De Santis, believed that "the importance of this incident in causing Blaine's defeat has been exaggerated."[12]

The American Protective Association (APA), the newest anti-Catholic group, was organized in Clinton, Iowa, in 1887. Its avowedly political aims were to oppose any Catholic candidates or Catholic political influence. The APA specialized in bogus papal encyclicals and lurid scare stories about arsenals in Catholic cathedrals, convents, churches, and schools. Virtual hysteria erupted in isolated rural areas where gossip was gospel.[13] The APA proved to be something of a flash in the pan, for, though it carried many communities in Nebraska, Iowa, Illinois, Michigan, and Ohio in 1892 and 1894, it soon dissipated and vanished from the political scene. Where it was a factor, it tended to work with and be absorbed by the Republican Party.[14]

In 1892 a minor religious issue caused some strife.

The Catholic Church had been the primary educator of many Indians in the Western states, and its Indian reservation schools received some public funding under a contract of 1869. Under this arrangement the church furnished buildings, board, lodging, and clothing for the students, while the government allowed a fixed annual per capita compensation. The Bureau of Catholic Indian Missions acted as liaison with the Government. Though the project began under a Republican administration, Democrat Grover Cleveland increased federal appropriations from $65,220 in 1884 to $347,672 in 1889. The Presbyterians, who maintained a few schools, received $41,825. The Republican Presidential victory of 1888 augured some changes.

President Benjamin Harrison named General Thomas J. Morgan, a Baptist minister, to the post of Indian commissioner, and Dr. Daniel Dorchester, a noted Methodist preacher and author, to the position of Commissioner of Indian Education. Morgan promptly announced that he would withdraw government aid from the religious schools. Morgan then dismissed Catholics who were serving in the Indian office. Dorchester, who had written a savage book *Romanism Versus the Public School System* in 1888, fired almost all Catholic teachers. Catholics were outraged but were unable to reverse the policies.

President Harrison, though he admitted that he had voted the Know-Nothing ticket, claimed to be sympathetic to the Catholic Church's "stand with regard to the social order, obedience to authority, and temperance without fanaticism."[15] Harrison reiterated his opposition to religious prejudice, but refused to overrule Morgan and Dorchester, whose confirmation by the Senate had been approved only 28–16.

Harry J. Sievers believes that this issue "resulted in an apparently heavy Catholic vote against President Harrison in 1892."[16] Harrison was defeated by ex-President

Cleveland, and much of the Catholic press exulted. *The Courier* of Ogdensburg, New York, declared it "a great Catholic victory," while the *Catholic Herald* of New York remarked: "The Republican Party, led by bigots, invaded the sanctuary of the home, usurped parental rights, and robbed the Catholic Indians of their only treasure, their faith; but the people, true to the best traditions of America, hurled it from power. Cleveland's victory was, in truth, the defeat of bigotry."

No religious issues surfaced in the exciting Bryan-McKinley election of 1896, though William Jennings Bryan was a fundamentalist-prohibitionist, whose views would have little appeal to Catholics, Jews, and many European Protestants. The 1896 election was a major "realigning" election as the urban areas throughout the country, and the East in general, swung overwhelmingly to William McKinley. Though the nation's heaviest 100 or so Catholic counties gave Bryan 57%, he lost many German Catholic strongholds in Wisconsin (the first time the Democrats lost there).[17]

Historian De Santis places the Civil War elections in historical perspective. "Catholicism was dragged into practically every presidential election in the post-Civil War generation. Yet as an issue it played a minor and subordinate role, and never came close to being a determining factor in the outcome of any one of these contests."[18]

In 1908, William Howard Taft, a Unitarian, was attacked as an infidel by some fundamentalist preachers. Taft replied that the Unitarians of this country could accept and bear the prejudice, but he wondered whether a country professing religious freedom could do so. President Theodore Roosevelt was irked by the injection of religious issues, and responded archly, "If there is one thing for which we stand in this country, it is for complete religious freedom, and it is an emphatic negation of this right to cross-examine a man on his religious views before being willing to support him for office."[19]

Taft received the brunt of anti-Catholic smears because he was civil governor of the Philippines when the U.S. Government compensated some friars for land expropriated by American authorities. Taft was called a tool of the Vatican.

Woodrow Wilson was free from religious questioning, though some fundamentalists attacked his appointment of Louis Brandeis, the first Jewish Supreme Court justice, and his meeting with Pope Benedict XV at the Vatican during his triumphal tour of Europe.

On Thanksgiving Day, 1915, on the top of Stone Mountain, near Atlanta, Georgia, the infamous Knights of the Ku Klux Klan was reconstituted. Its bêtes noires were Catholics, Jews, and Negroes. It was sworn to uphold Anglo-Saxon Protestant civilization. The Invisible Empire soon grew to frightening strength and disgraced American life for decades to come. By 1924 it was reliably estimated to have 4 or 5 million members, being strongest in Indiana, Ohio, and Texas. Considerable support was given the Klan by Protestant clergy. Of the 39 "national lecturers" employed by the Klan from 1922 to 1928, 26 were Protestant ministers. Of 241 pamphleteers and agitators used by the Klan, 110 were preachers.[20]

Other anti-Catholic militants included the Guardians of Liberty, founded by Georgia politician Tom Watson, who spewed forth a torrent of bigotry from his Jeffersonian Publishing Company in Thomson, Georgia; the Knights of Luther; the *Menace,* published in Aurora, Missouri, and claiming over one million readers in its heyday; the Rail Splitter Press in Milan, Illinois, under the aegis of the redoutable William Lloyd Clark, who called himself "an anti-Papal propagandist"; the Protestant Guards of Washington, D.C.; and *The Protestant,* a monthly journal founded by Gilbert O. Nations, Ph.D., a scholarly sophisticated bigot who sought the Presidency in 1924 and wrote such books as *Rome in Congress* and *Roman Catholic War on Public Schools.*

There was a mild religious boom, oddly enough, during the jazz age. Presbyterians, Lutherans, and Baptists gained over a million new members between 1916 and 1926. Episcopalians almost doubled from 1.1 million to 1.9 million. The feared Roman Catholic Church increased from 15.7 to 18.6 million.[21] Dulce and Richter wrote: "Revivalism, the World War, and the spectacular growth of the Roman Catholic Church had caused a dramatic upturn in church-going. In 1880, 20 per cent of the population attended church; by 1930 the figure was 47 per cent. America also counted another hundred religious sects and an additional 50,000 church buildings."[22]

3

The Al Smith Campaign

The story of the Al Smith campaign of 1928 has been retold many times. This is only a brief sketch of its religious implications, for it was a watershed election in American history.

Alfred E. Smith, whose forebears came from Ireland, was born on the Lower East Side of New York in 1873. His formal education ended before he completed the ninth grade, when he had to quit school to help support his family. He had a natural inclination for politics and soon entered into its rough-and-tumble arena in New York City. In 1904 he was elected to the New York State Assembly and served there until 1915. He later became sheriff of New York County, president of the board of aldermen of New York City, and governor of New York in 1918. He was defeated in the Republican landslide of 1920, but reelected in 1922, 1924, and 1926. His record was considered relatively progressive and much in tune with the needs of his urban constituents.

His record on religious affairs was somewhat mixed. In 1915 he offered an amendment to the Commissioner of Education at the New York State Constitutional Convention that would have eliminated the state ban on aid to parochial schools. As governor he continued the practice of supplying four million dollars a year in state aid to parochial schools. He was also somewhat naive about the public relations consequences of his public religious life. He made several well-publicized trips to the Vatican, where Pope Pius XI effusively praised him. He had a picture of Pope Pius XI hanging in the governor's mansion in Albany and he made an appearance at the 1926 Eucharistic Congress in Chicago, where he is supposed to have kissed a cardinal's ring, provoking an angry outburst from Methodist Bishop Adna W. Leonard, who said, "No governor can kiss the papal ring and get within gun shot of the White House."[1]

On the other hand, Smith appointed excellent men to the state cabinet, including a reasonable balance of Protestants, Catholics, and Jews. He approved a bill extending the grounds for divorce which the Catholic Church opposed. He objected to most forms of public censorship, though he signed the so-called Padlock Bill of 1927, which provided for the closing of any theaters for an entire year if any play presented was declared indecent by the courts. He also reorganized state government and supported social welfare and public education. He denounced the Lusk Committee, which was an early un-American activities committee seeking Communists in the New York state government. He won the admiration of many liberals and intellectuals.

In a sense the 1928 campaign began in 1924, as Smith was one of the two leading contenders for the Democratic Presidential nomination. His opponent was former Secretary of the Treasury William G. McAdoo, who represented the Protestant-prohibitionist rural wing of the party. Smith represented the urban anti-prohibitionist and largely Catholic and Jewish segments of the party. The Democratic convention was so bitterly divided that it narrowly defeated a resolution condemning the Ku Klux Klan and then could not make up its mind whether to nominate Smith or McAdoo. On the 103d ballot, the weary delegates finally settled on a dull, colorless Wall

Street lawyer from West Virginia, John W. Davis. The liberals were angry at the party's failure to break with the Bryan-populist tradition and deserted the party in droves to support the candidacy of "Fighting Bob" La Follette of Wisconsin. The Democrats received the lowest vote in their entire history—less than 29% of the national total—and carried no states outside of the South. Smith was reelected governor of New York handily and began preparing for the 1928 campaign.

The first serious discussion of the religious issue arose in 1927, when Charles C. Marshall, a scholarly Episcopalian lawyer and a self-proclaimed admirer of the Roman Catholic Church, published his "Open Letter to Governor Alfred E. Smith" in the April 1927 issue of *Atlantic Monthly.* Marshall had spent years studying Catholicism and professed a "love for the Latin church." Nevertheless he was seriously concerned about Vatican policy on the relationship of church and state and its historic hostility to religious liberty. Did such policies demand a dual loyalty among prospective Roman Catholic public servants in a democratic non-Catholic society? He questioned whether Smith could be sufficiently independent of the various papal encyclicals on church-state relations. He worried about whether religious harmony and peace could be preserved if there were constant church-state antagonisms. It was a thoughtful and serious article and Governor Smith agreed to reply in the May 1927 issue of the same journal.

Smith, who is alleged to have said, after reading Marshall's article, "What the hell is a papal encyclical?" (revealing his rather limited knowledge of Catholicism), asked Father Patrick Duffy, the famous World War I chaplain, and a young priest, Francis J. Spellman, later to become cardinal, to help him prepare a response. Smith's response did not really answer most of the questions Marshall raised but pledged that he was a loyal

American, a genuine patriot, and a true Catholic at the same time. He professed strong support for separation of church and state and public education. He wrote: "I believe in the support of the public school as one of the cornerstones of American liberty. I believe in the right of every parent to choose whether his child shall be educated in the public school or in a religious school, supported by those of his own faith."

Unfortunately, this was to be the only rational discussion of the religious issue for the next year and a half. Most Roman Catholics objected to Smith's even being asked to respond to Marshall, and most Roman Catholic periodicals refused to discuss the issues Marshall raised. On the other hand, Protestant extremists refused to accept Smith's guarantee of good faith and began a long campaign to preserve their dominance over American public life and to keep the White House closed to Roman Catholics.

Though Smith had written in his *Atlantic Monthly* article that he recognized "no power in the institutions of my church to interfere with the operations of the Constitution of the United States or the enforcement of the law of the land," millions of Protestants refused to believe him. When Smith had written, "I believe in absolute freedom of conscience for all men and in equality of all churches, all sects, and all beliefs before the law as a matter of right and not as a matter of favor," Protestants pointed to papal encyclicals that said just the opposite.

Much of the religious issue was *sub rosa*. Edmund Moore has written that "anti-Catholicism was indeed the silent issue in the national press and was very much more significant than the somewhat meager news or editorial space assigned to it would indicate."[2] Senator Tom Heflin of Alabama, a frock-coated demagogue, made violent anti-Catholic speeches on the floor of Congress. He denounced the Catholic Church in no uncertain terms and even urged on one occasion that Catholics be deported from the country. In him was combined social, cultural, and theological bigotry, and it remains incredible to see how any civilized society could have elected such a man to the U.S. Senate. The writings of Tom Watson, a Georgia fanatic, flooded the country. Anti-Catholic books were issued from a variety of presses, such as the Jeffersonian Publishing Company in Thomson, Georgia, and the Rail Splitter Press in Milan, Illinois, whose flamboyant leader, William Lloyd Clark, made a public career out of anti-popery.

Tons of salacious and vulgar propaganda—accounts of ex-nuns and priests, secret conspiracies to invade the United States, to burn Protestant Bibles and slay all Protestants—like the bogus Knights of Columbus oath, circulated throughout the country, especially in the rural areas of the South and in the border states.

Many Protestant clergy were deeply involved in the fight against Smith. Methodists and Baptists tended to dominate, though even Unitarians, like Dr. Albert C. Dieffenbach, editor of *Christian Register,* questioned Smith's ability to be President and reminded Unitarians of previous Catholic persecutions. As Moore wrote, "Though there were more Baptists than Methodists in the South, it is a Methodist bishop, James Cannon, who will be remembered as the driving force in organizing the battle of Southern Protestantism against Al Smith. Bishop Cannon, more than any one else, was probably responsible for the failure of the Democratic Party to hold the line for Smith in the upper South and in Texas and Florida."[3] A number of other Methodist ministers joined the fray, although one bishop, Warren A. Candler of Atlanta, opposed the politicization of the Methodist Church.

Religious journals joined the religious leaders in the attack on Smith, though several studies indicate that it was as much support for Prohibition as opposition to Catholicism that led various Protestant organizations and magazines editorially to endorse Herbert Hoover. *Christian Century,* for example, one of the most respected liberal Protestant journals, was so committed to Prohibition that it stated that it would oppose anyone who opposed enforcement of the Prohibition amendment. The Methodist Board of Temperance and Public Morals was a major factor in the defeat of Smith, but its rationale was certainly more Prohibition than religion. Many Lutheran and Presbyterian editors opposed Smith with considerable boldness.

Some of the attacks on Smith bordered on the obscene and vile and certainly went beyond the line of decency and the role that religious leaders should play in society. For example, Rev. Mordecai Fowler Ham, an itinerant evangelist and onetime pastor of First Baptist Church in Oklahoma City, told a congregation, "If you vote for Al Smith, you're voting against Christ and you'll all be damned."[4] Dr. John Roach Straton, a militant fundamentalist and pastor of Calvary Baptist Church in New York City, spent literally months campaigning all over the country against Smith, telling his listeners that no Christian could possibly vote for Al Smith, that "hell's forces were on Smith's side and that Smith is the nominee of the worst forces of hell." Among other Protestant clergymen Dr. Ed Bywater of Riverside Park, New York, delivered again and again a popular sermon entitled "To Hell with the Pope."

A once-popular evangelist, Billy Sunday, called Smith's supporters "damnable whiskey politicians, bootleggers, crooks, pimps and street walkers."[5] Violent attacks on Catholics and Catholicism appeared in the fundamentalist *Fellowship Forum, The Protestant,* and dozens of other lurid underground magazines.

The Republican Party was not completely immune

from occasionally indulging in some anti-Catholicism for political gain. Mrs. Willie W. Caldwell, a Virginia National Committeewoman, wrote to the women in her state, saying: "Mr. Hoover himself and the National Committee are depending on the women to save our country in this hour of very vital moral religious crisis. We must save the United States from being Romanized and rum-ridden, and the call is to the women to do something." Her letter outraged many Democrats and liberal Republicans. Republican officials in Florida and North Carolina distributed anti-Catholic literature. Perhaps the worst violator was Mrs. Mabel Walker Willebrandt, an assistant attorney general assigned to Prohibition enforcement. On September 7 she spoke to a delegation of Methodists in the Ohio Methodist Conference in Springfield, Ohio, and made a none-too-subtle appeal for religious bloc votes. She said: "There are two thousand pastors here. You have in your churches more than six hundred thousand members of the Methodist Church in Ohio alone. That is enough to swing the election."[6]

To his credit, Republican nominee Herbert Hoover denounced the Caldwell letter and made some appeals for religious harmony. In his memoirs published after the campaign, however, Hoover blamed Smith for introducing the religious issue in the public arena by Smith's famous September 20 address before a rather hostile crowd in Oklahoma City. This seems rather absurd of Hoover, since the religious issue was the most emotional and most widely discussed issue in the entire campaign. Smith faced the crowd at Oklahoma City and lashed out at his enemies as bigots. He said that no one had a right to question his religion, that he was a loyal and patriotic American, and that his cabinet had had ten Protestants, one Jew, and only three Catholics. He talked about "the wicked motive of religious intolerance" and said that "no decent right-minded, upstanding American citizen can for a moment countenance the shower of lying statements, with no basis in fact, that has been reduced to printed matter and sent broadcast through the mails of this country." Smith went on to say: "I here emphatically declare that I do not wish any member of my faith in any part of the United States to vote for me on any religious grounds. I want them to vote for me only when in their hearts and consciences they become convinced that my election will promote the best interests of our country. By the same token, I cannot refrain from saying that any person who votes against me simply because of my religion is not, to my way of thinking, a good citizen. Let me remind the Democrats of this country that we belong to the party of Thomas Jefferson, whose proudest boast was that he was the author of the Virginia Statute for Religious Freedom. Let me remind the citizens of every political faith that his Statute of Religious Freedom has become a part of the sacred heritage of our land."[7]

The reaction to Governor Smith's address was predictable. His sympathizers, like the *New York Times,* defended his courage while Republican papers like the *New York Herald Tribune* accused Smith of injecting the religious issue into the campaign. Several Republicans, for example, Nicholas Longworth, Speaker of the House of Representatives, and former Governor Henry J. Allen of Kansas, claimed that Smith had "cast the first stone of religious intolerance in Oklahoma City."[8] Such charges seem ridiculous from the vantage point of today.

One final observation should be made regarding the campaign. There was a type of cultural snobbishness, a subconscious belief that only Protestants were good Americans, which influenced the outcome of the 1928 election. There was a sizable segment of the electorate, not explicitly anti-Catholic, which believed that there was just something wrong with a non-Anglo-Saxon Protestant in the White House. It just wasn't seemly that a man from the Lower East Side of New York should aspire to the highest office of the land. William Allen White, "the Sage of Emporia" and a noted popular Republican columnist, wrote, "It is not that Governor Smith is a Catholic and a wet which makes him an offense to the villagers and town dwellers, . . . the whole Puritan civilization which has built a sturdy, orderly nation is threatened by Smith."[9] *American Issue,* a magazine of the Anti-Saloon League, was even more blatant. It said: "Hoover represents the stately, reliable, dependable civilization which has built America and maintained its high standards. . . . Smith appeals to the sporty, jazz and liberal elements of our population. He is not in harmony with the principles of our forefathers. If you believe in Anglo-Saxon Protestant domination; if you believe in the maintenance of that civilization founded by our Puritan ancestors, and preserved by our fathers, . . . you will vote for Hoover rather than Smith."[10]

Not all Protestants joined the anti-Smith crusade. Scholarly Presbyterian clergyman and author Dr. Henry van Dyke denounced the bigotry against Smith and warmly defended the New York governor. Van Dyke criticized the Moderator of the Presbyterian General Assembly, Dr. Hugh Walker, who had urged all Presbyterians to fight "to the bitter end the election of Alfred E. Smith." A group of moderate Protestants and Catholics, concerned about the long-range effects of the religious prejudice in the 1928 election, founded the Calvert Associates. One of the leaders of this group was Dr. Ralph Adams Cram, celebrated architect of the Episcopal Cathedral of St. John the Divine, and the prominent Roman Catholic editor of *Commonweal,* Michael Williams. This group wrote letters to the press, ran newspaper advertisements countering the unfair attacks on the Catholic Church, and arranged for liberal Protestants like Dr. van

Dyke to speak against religious bigotry. Many Protestant clergymen spoke out against the smear campaign against Smith, as did Dr. Nicholas Murray Butler, president of Columbia University, Dr. S. Parkes Cadman, president of the Federal Council of the Churches of Christ in America, and Methodist Bishop Warren A. Candler. They were somewhat of a minority within their respective religious communities, but one result of the Smith campaign was the foundation of the National Conference of Christians and Jews in 1928 to "promote justice, amity and understanding between the many groups that comprise America." It should be noted also that many individual Protestant laymen bitterly resented the political rallies held in churches. Many people booed, heckled, or walked out when preachers like Dr. Straton and others spoke at their local meetings. One woman is reported to have said, "I came to hear the gospel preached, not politics" and stalked out of one of the anti-Smith meetings.

The closing days of the campaign saw an intensification of the religious issue. Rev. Bob Schuler, pastor of Trinity Methodist Church in Los Angeles, broadcast on nationwide radio, in which he charged that Roman Catholics had murdered Presidents Lincoln, Garfield, and McKinley and that all the political assassinations in the world were carried out by Catholics. Methodist bishop Horace M. DuBose, one of the leaders of the anti-Smith Democrats in the South, claimed that out of 8,500 Southern Methodist preachers only four were supporting Smith. Dr. Gilbert Nations in his journal *The Protestant* blared a front-page editorial entitled "Smith Must Be Annihilated." In Florida colorful former Governor Sydney J. Catts charged that Catholic churches were arsenals of guns and dynamite ready to take over the country if Smith were elected. Catts warned that all Catholic churches had basements with ammunition stored ready for the final takeover and a massacre of heretics. Catts was one of the most flamboyant Southern politicians in this period. He had been elected governor in 1916 on an anti-Catholic platform and his billboards proclaimed rather immodestly, "The poor man has only three friends: Sears Roebuck, Jesus Christ, and Sydney J. Catts."[11]

Catholics were bitterly hurt and dismayed by the introduction of the religious issue into the campaign, but a study of Catholic periodicals found almost none had supported their coreligionist officially.[12] This was in stark contrast, of course, to the Protestant publications' strong support for Hoover. Smith and his advisers, however, were not completely blameless in the way they handled the religious issue. Smith appointed John J. Raskob, a conservative Catholic millionaire from Delaware, as chairman of the National Democratic Committee. It probably would have been wiser to have appointed a more neutral figure, but Smith was apparently unaware of the deep suspicion with which he was regarded. David Burner expresses a view that is more widely accepted today: "For if he could not shirk his religion itself, or modify the slightest symbolic act of allegiance, he could have at least addressed himself more fully to the fears in which so many of his fellow Americans had been reared. . . . Smith might have acknowledged the occasional alliance between Latin Catholicism and political tyranny and then pointed to the historical American tradition of religious harmony, as embodied in Lord Baltimore; he and his supporters might even have made explicit contrast between their position, along with the position of countless of their fellow religionists in the United States, and that of Catholic reactionaries; he might have sought out the support of Protestant clergymen or outstanding laymen; he might have increased the Protestant contingent in his campaign committee. In short, Smith might have acted as though he was aware of the anxiety, however silly or bigoted, that was felt by much of rural American Protestantism, as one who shared with it a sense of America's role in preserving religious liberty."[13] Dr. James H. Smylie, in his trenchant essay "The Roman Catholic Church, The State and Al Smith" (*Church History,* September 1960), found a kernel of hopefulness in the rather unfortunate campaign. "Roman Catholics were slandered; of this there is no shadow of a doubt. But there is evidence that Roman Catholics themselves invited, indeed, provoked, in their own writings a discussion of the relationship between the church and the state in America. During the 1928 campaign, some Americans raised questions about the feasibility of a Roman Catholic president in an attempt to come to terms with one of the most crucial and continuing problems in American life."

We shall look at the structure of the vote in the 1928 campaign in the next chapter, but the defeat of Al Smith, though painful and disillusioning to many, may have paved the way to important political changes in American life. Though many Catholics, including the editor of the *Catholic World,* called Smith a martyr and claimed that his defeat proved that there was a religious test in American politics, there is evidence that no Protestant could have defeated Hoover in 1928. The prosperity of the country, the immense prestige of Herbert Hoover, and the divided condition of the Democratic Party rendered the election of a Democrat unlikely. Al Smith was a precursor for the realignment of American politics during the New Deal. Richard Hofstadter writes: "Even in his losing campaign Smith turned the normally huge Republican pluralities in the twelve largest cities into a slender Democratic plurality. He brought into the voting stream of the Democratic Party ethnic groups that had never taken part in politics and others that had been mainly

Republican. He extricated his party from its past dependence on agrarian interests and made it known to the great urban populations. He lost a campaign that had to be lost, but in such a way as to restore his party as an effective opposition and to pave the way for the victories of F.D.R."[14]

4

Religious Factors in the 1928 Vote

There was a record turnout on Election Day, 1928. More than 36 million Americans went to the polls, compared to fewer than 29 million in 1924. The heaviest vote increases occurred in states where the religious issue was raging (Florida, New Jersey, Massachusetts, Pennsylvania, Louisiana, Virginia). Al Smith was buried by Hoover, 21.4 million–15.0 million in popular vote, 444–87 in electoral vote. Compared to 1924, Hoover gained 5.7 million votes, but, significantly, Smith gained 6.6 million and received the highest Democratic vote ever recorded. In fact, only Hoover, Harding, and Coolidge had topped his vote.

Smith won 122 counties that had never gone Democratic before. He won a plurality of 38,000 in the twelve largest cities, which the Democrats lost badly in 1920 and 1924. A careful analysis of these counties reveals that all are predominantly or substantially Catholic.

Smith's increase was concentrated in certain counties. Yet Smith gained in 2,080 counties, while actually losing votes in 997 counties. Smith's vote percentage varied widely, with serious declines registered in the South and the border states. There was no direct correlation, however, between the Catholic percentage of the population and the increase in the Smith vote. Heavily Catholic New Mexico, the third heaviest Catholic state at that time,

49

went strongly for Hoover. South Carolina, Mississippi, and Arkansas, having almost an absence of Catholics, remained loyal to the Democratic Party.

The most we can say is that religion influenced the vote in certain areas where the local religious climate somehow affected the outcome. Let us look at certain states.

In Pennsylvania, religious voting was as severe as anywhere in the nation. Heavily Catholic Republican Elk County gave Smith 59.5%, while Protestant Democratic York County gave him only 19.7%. Five counties gave Smith a gain of 20% or more of the total vote. Collectively, they are the state's heaviest Catholic counties, ranging from 35.4% to 56.6% Catholic in the total population. Among church members 77% are Catholic, only 23% Protestant. Conversely, in 18 counties Smith ran more than 10% behind the vote given to Democrat Davis in 1924. Four normally Democratic counties (Columbia, Fulton, Greene, and Monroe) went for Hoover by a landslide. Though Smith lost badly in Pennsylvania, his vote in the Catholic counties increased more heavily than the anti-Catholic vote.

Anti-Catholic voting was pronounced in New Jersey, Maryland, Ohio, Tennessee, and West Virginia. Smith ran 10% to 27% behind the normal Democratic vote in 4 counties in New Jersey, 8 in Maryland, 5 in Ohio, 3 in Tennessee, and 4 in West Virginia—all of which were heavily evangelical Protestant. In counties where many of the smaller sects abound, Smith was buried. The Democratic percentage of the vote declined 42% in Houston County, Tennessee, and 26% in Holmes County, Ohio.

My research on religion and voting in 1928 tends to confirm the previous studies, though I think that religion and Prohibition were so intermingled in most voters' minds that the two issues were mutually reinforcing. Referenda on Prohibition in 1917 in Iowa and in 1926 in New York demonstrated that most Catholics were anti-Prohibition and WASP's pro-Prohibition. But Catholics were heavily Democratic and WASP's Republican, so their 1928 vote was not unexpected. A number of sophisticated voter studies, such as the Ogburn-Talbot analysis that appeared in *Social Forces* (December 1929), concluded that Prohibition was a more significant predictor of voter choice in 1928 than religious affiliation. A convincing demonstration of religious influences on voting might have occurred if the 1928 *Republican* candidate had been Catholic and anti-Prohibition, and the Democratic nominee had been Protestant and pro-Prohibition. Then, a massive realignment could have been a real possibility. For this reason I have saved most of the detailed precinct analysis of religious voting for the 1960 Kennedy campaign, when the religious issue *alone* was not clouded by other factors.

There is a relationship between Prohibition sentiment, religious affiliation, and the Smith vote in New York and Iowa. New Yorkers voted almost 3 to 1 to repeal Prohibition in a 1926 referendum, although several counties voted to maintain the "noble experiment." The six heaviest Prohibition counties were the six most anti-Smith counties and the heaviest Protestant ones.

Iowa's 1917 Prohibition referendum is a classic study of religious/political voting. The state has three basic religious blocs: Roman Catholics (30%), Lutherans (23.9%), and WASP's, native American Protestants who are members of the Baptist, Methodist, and Disciples of Christ churches (27.4%). There is some justification for including Congregationalists (UCC) and Presbyterians in the WASP category, which would then total 37.8%.

On Prohibition, WASP's were the sole fervent supporters of the referendum, which narrowly lost 215,625 to 214,963. The 7 counties most heavily WASP collectively voted 72.9% for it. Lutherans divided according to ethnic identity. German Lutherans in Bremer County voted solidly 72% no, but Scandinavians in Worth and Winnebago counties voted 52% and 65% yes, respectively. Scandinavians emphasized teetotaling and a more puritanical approach to life, and were almost indistinguishable from WASP's. Roman Catholics cast almost 80% against Prohibition.

In the 1928 election Roman Catholics understandably cast a large 65% for Smith, compared to 36.7% in WASP counties and 36.0% in Lutheran counties. German Lutherans gave Smith almost 45%, but Scandinavians gave him less than 30%. Interestingly, in 6 of the 7 WASP counties, Smith ran better than the pro-Prohibition vote, but in German Lutheran and Reformed areas he ran 27% behind. Traditional party loyalties obviously played a role, since many WASP's are Democrats and many Lutherans, Republicans.[1]

Another way of verifying the religious impact on the Presidential vote is to look at certain counties that reflect religious homogeneity. We have already seen the existence of heavy pro-Smith and anti-Smith voting and determined that a great deal of it must have been related solely to religion.

The 106 heaviest Roman Catholic counties in the United States went rather comfortably for Smith, though not as heavily as one might expect. The 15 urban counties, which had been solidly Republican since 1896, went for Smith 52.6%–47.4%. The small-town–rural counties, where there is more homogeneity, gave Smith 58.5%. (In the 20 heaviest Catholic counties, where over 70% of the population is Catholic, Smith won 60.0%.) Some of the gains were impressive and were noted previously.

It is a truism in politics that the smaller the voting unit, the more meaningful and reliable will be the data. Though much of the precinct data for 1928 is not available, and little accurate religious data are available for small areas, some evidence exists of overwhelming Catholic support for Smith. Irish Catholics in New York gave Smith 82% and Italian Catholic New Yorkers gave him 77%. Polish Catholics in Chicago recorded 83% for Smith, while Italians in Boston gave him an all-time high 95%.[2] Probably the best estimate for Smith among Catholic voters nationwide is 85% to 90%.

There are 34 counties in the Midwest (17 in Minnesota, 9 in North Dakota, 3 in Iowa, 2 in Nebraska, 2 in South Dakota, 1 in Wisconsin), where Lutherans are more than 50% of the total population. These counties went 63% for Hoover. In 1924, La Follette and Coolidge ran about even, so Smith lost ground somewhat, though his showing was quite respectable compared to Woodrow Wilson and William Jennings Bryan. Another 25 counties are 45% to 50% Lutheran today, many of them having Lutheran majorities in the 1926 census. In these counties Smith ran a bit better, receiving 38.5%.

One scholarly analysis of Lutheran voting in 1928 appeared in Douglas C. Stange's "Al Smith and the Republican Party at Prayer: The Lutheran Vote—1928" (*Review of Politics*, July 1970). In it Stange concluded: "First of all, antagonism toward the Democratic standard bearer, Al Smith, was very real. Although Lutherans frequently voiced the all-American cry for preserving the separation of church and state, they were politically involved in indirectly favoring Hoover by their discussion of Smith's religion. Only the very naive could read the Lutheran press and fail to get the message that Hoover was the man Lutherans should elect.

"Secondly, although Smith had the bulk of the Lutheran press against him, a number of Lutherans defended him, a courageous action in view of Smith's unpopularity in Lutheran circles. That these men gained some converts to Smith's cause seems to be evidenced by the showing the Governor made in some Lutheran areas."

There are 96 heavily Baptist counties in the South and in the border states where anti-Smith voting was enormous. Previous comfortable Democratic majorities above 60% evaporated as Hoover beat Smith 59%–41% in these strongly prohibitionist Bible Belt counties. Methodist strongholds in Kansas, West Virginia, and Maryland also swung heavily Republican, giving Hoover about 65%. (See Appendix, Table 19.)

Most American Jews considered the Republican Party the more progressive from 1856 to 1928. With the one exception of Wilson in 1916, Jews gave GOP Presidential candidates a majority of their votes. In 1924, however, the popularity of Progressive Robert La Follette deprived Coolidge of a majority. He won only a plurality. The turning point came in 1928.

The vindictive attacks on Smith, Catholicism, and foreign-born Americans angered America's Jews. Viewing themselves as barely tolerated underdogs, they instinctively sympathized with Governor Smith. Smith's progressive record as New York's governor, where half of the nation's Jews resided, and his appointment of Jews to high state office further solidified Jewish support.[3] Jewish concern for urban values and resentment at Prohibition and anti-immigration laws obliterated in one election their historic Republicanism. Never again would a majority of Jews pull a Republican Presidential lever. The swing to Smith was astounding. In Boston's Ward 14, where *78%* of the voters were registered Republicans, *61%* voted for Smith. Fully *half* of the Republican Jews voted for Smith. In four New York assembly districts, where Davis received one of three votes in 1924, Smith received 66% to 71%. In Chicago's Ward 24, Smith amassed 74.5%.[4] Al Smith began a Jewish exodus from the Republican Party which was accelerated and completed by Franklin Roosevelt and Adlai Stevenson.

The exodus shows up even on the Congressional level. In 1920, of the eleven Jews elected to Congress, ten were Republicans, and one a Socialist. By 1930, six were Democrats and only two, Republicans.

Several conclusions emerge from this study of the 1928 vote. Catholics, Jews, and many European Protestants voted for Smith. Native American Protestants voted heavily for Hoover. There appears to be no correlation between denomination and vote. The percentage of Catholics correlates highly with the Smith vote only when *it is sufficiently large* (e.g., 40% or more). Below that level, the anti-Smith vote was sometimes heavy in counties having almost no Catholics, but it was also significant in counties where Catholics were a substantial minority. Perhaps Protestants felt threatened by a growing Catholic population, and the ensuing rivalry produced increased anti-Catholicism. On the other hand, Protestants living in all-Protestant counties may not have feared Catholic rivalry and thus were unlikely to vote against Smith. Similarly, Baptist and Lutheran strongholds were not necessarily more anti-Smith than pluralistic areas where many Protestant churches were visible.

How significant was the religious issue? Was Ogburn right in maintaining that Prohibition was three times more important than religion in determining the 1928 vote? Could a Protestant have beaten Hoover?

Richard Hofstadter, said, "There was no Protestant alive who could have beaten Hoover in 1928."[5] Edmund Moore believes that a Protestant Democrat would probably not have run as well as Smith.[6] On the other hand, Smith himself, his running mate Senator Joseph Robinson of Arkansas, Mark Sullivan, Wilbur Cash, Bernard Baruch, *Time,* the *New York Times,* and many others attributed Smith's defeat primarily to religious prejudice. Nebraska's maverick Senator George Norris, a Republican who endorsed Smith, stated: "The greatest element involved in the landslide was religion. Regret it and conceal it as we may, religion had more to do with the defeat of Governor Smith than any other one thing."[7] Historian David Burner concluded, "There is . . . reason to believe that religion outweighed prohibition as an election issue."[8] I tend to agree. I do not think a Protestant would have defeated Hoover, but it would have been closer.

5

From Smith to Kennedy

Blatant religious issues were absent from Presidential campaigns for three decades. Though the voting behavior of religious groups fluctuated during the 1932–1960 period, there was no focal point for their national expression. All that was changed when another prominent Roman Catholic sought the nation's highest office.

On a personal level Protestant-Catholic relations generally improved during the depression and the war years, though the official institutional churches were still quite aloof and distrustful of each other. The Roman Catholic Church continued to gain in membership and in corresponding political and social influence. Buttressed by many notable conversions, it progressed substantially "to make America Catholic." Protestants were wary and rather uncertain of the ultimate goals of their traditional rival.

A deterioration in relationships began after World War II. Protestants accused the Roman Catholic hierarchy of placing pressure on the U.S. State Department to deny visas to Protestant missionaries to South America. Repeated harassment of Protestants in such Catholic lands as Spain and Colombia added to the distrust. The Vatican officially frowned on the burgeoning ecumenical movement, rejecting Catholic participation on any official level. It refused to send Catholic delegates to the inaugural sessions of the World Council of Churches in Amsterdam in 1948. Papal encyclicals, beginning especially with *Mortalium Animos* (1928, Pius XI), called on Protestants, Anglicans, and Orthodox heretics and schismatics to return to the ancient mother church of Christendom.

Furthermore, Roman Catholics were demanding public aid for their schools and hospitals as a matter of distributive justice and fair public policy, thus creating a new wedge in interfaith relationships. Paul Blanshard's provocative and widely read *American Freedom and Catholic Power* articulated the deep-rooted fears of many Protestants and liberals. John Cogley, then a liberal Catholic journalist, admits in his *Catholic America* that "over the years there were enough examples of the use of Catholic power to unsettle any liberal dedicated to freedom of thought and expression who might be uncertain about the Church's ultimate aims. . . . The liberals' case against Catholicism was founded on solid fact and easy to document."[1]

In hotly contested referenda in Massachusetts in 1946 and 1948 organized Catholic efforts successfully maintained a legal ban on birth control. Against what was perceived as a militant and aggressive policy of proselytism and political influence Protestants and Other Americans United was organized as a counterforce.

Catholics countered by claiming that they had a constitutional right to seek both expanding political influence and larger church membership. They claimed that much of contemporary Protestantism was desiccated, devoid of spiritual authority and certainty. One of their spokesmen, James M. O'Neill, in his *Catholicism and American Freedom*, acquitted Catholics of the charges made by Blanshard. He contended that Catholicism's emphasis on authority independent of the state would strengthen democracy and freedom and prevent socialism and communism. O'Neill also maintained that Catholic members of Congress and the Catholic electorate in general were divided along conservative-liberal and Democratic-Republican lines just like the other religions and did not constitute a disloyal clericalist bloc.

President Harry S. Truman's decision to appoint Mark W. Clark as official U.S. ambassador to the Vatican on October 20, 1951, rather than as a personal representative (as FDR had done with Myron C. Taylor) provoked an unexpected fury from the Protestant community. Protestants charged that such an action would give preferential treatment to Catholicism and would violate the spirit, if not the letter, of the First Amendment. Mass protest meetings and a nationwide letter-writing campaign to Congress and the White House were so intense that General Clark, an Episcopalian, asked that his name be withdrawn on January 13, 1952. One sidelight to this nasty controversy was President Truman's pique at his personal pastor's sermon (Dr. Edward Hughes Pruden, of Washington's First Baptist Church) against the appointment. Truman intensely disliked meddling clerics and he never returned to services at First Baptist.

Most of the controversy was vituperative, though at least one scholar, Mark DeWolfe Howe of Harvard Law School, challenged the constitutionality of the appointment in his article "Diplomacy, Religion and the Constitution" (*Nation,* Jan. 12, 1952). Edwin S. Corwin of Princeton University and Arthur M. Schlesinger, Jr., of Harvard supported the nomination and ridiculed the opposition as nativists.[2] "On the whole," writes F. William O'Brien, "the secular press was favorably disposed toward having an American ambassador at the Vatican."[3] The *New York Times* and the *Washington Post* editorially endorsed the Truman appointment.

The National Council of Churches and the National

Association of Evangelicals (NAE) vigorously opposed the nomination. The NAE sent petitions to 8,000 churches on Reformation Sunday and reported spending $500,000 on radio time in three days in late October 1951.[4] The *Christian Century* (Oct. 31, 1951) warned senators that their vote on Clark's confirmation "will play a decisive role" in their political future. Methodist Bishop G. Bromley Oxnam even predicted in an Akron, Ohio, address that the Vatican ambassadorship "may well determine the 1952 election."[5] A Congregationalist pastor in Milwaukee, Rev. Stoddard Patterson, told his congregation to "vote for Protestants at the polls—Protestants who will uphold the Protestant traditions."[6]

The Catholic press supported the appointment on the grounds that the United States had a reliable ally in the Vatican in the struggle with world communism. Most Catholic spokesmen, though, clerical and lay, expressed dismay at the Protestant outburst and almost seemed willing to let the whole issue go away rather than to reawaken interfaith animosities.

Protestants won a major victory, so it seems, in this battle, though not without some eyebrow-raising at the methods engaged in by some of their leaders. *Christianity and Crisis* (Nov. 26, 1951) chided their fellow Protestants and said that many "seem so guided by emotion that they make a poor choice of issues for major emphasis." A nasty dispute in the late 1940's between Mrs. Eleanor Roosevelt and Francis Cardinal Spellman, the unofficial U.S. primate, over the question of public aid for parochial schools symbolized to many the growing divergence between liberal democracy and official Catholicism. The vehemence of the cardinal's attack on the revered widow of a beloved President shocked many Americans. His hat-in-hand apology at Hyde Park amused and relieved all but the most reactionary haters of Mrs. Roosevelt.

Protestant-Catholic relations were still strained through the 1950's, though more Catholics were elected to public office in non-Catholic strongholds (Edmund Muskie in Maine, Eugene McCarthy in Minnesota, etc.). Hostility to a Catholic President, which stood at 30% or more in polls throughout the 1940's and 1950's, declined to 25% in 1958 (34% among Protestants said that they would vote against a Catholic nominee of their party).

In 1956 two leading Roman Catholics, Massachusetts Senator John F. Kennedy and New York Mayor Robert F. Wagner, were considered strong contenders for the Democratic vice-presidential nomination, after Presidential aspirant Adlai E. Stevenson threw the vice-presidential nomination open to convention delegates. A secret "memorandum" prepared by Connecticut Democrat John Bailey was circulated among many party officials in an attempt to secure the nomination for a Catholic. It contended that millions of Catholic Democrats who liked Dwight D. Eisenhower in 1952 would return to the party if a Catholic were chosen as Stevenson's running mate. It was especially significant that Catholics were overwhelmingly concentrated in large population states with correspondingly large electoral votes. *U.S. News & World Report* summarized the essence of the Bailey argument as follows: "If he brought into the Democratic fold only those normally Democratic Catholics who voted for Ike, he could probably swing New York, Massachusetts, Rhode Island, Connecticut, Pennsylvania and Illinois—for 132 electoral votes. If he also wins the votes of Catholics who shifted to the Republicans in 1948 or earlier, he could also swing New Jersey, Minnesota, Michigan, California, Wisconsin, Ohio, Maryland, Montana, and maybe even New Hampshire—for a total of 265 electoral votes (needed to win: 266). Thus Ike could and would be defeated."[7]

When this strategy was revealed, the leading Protestant journal *Christian Century* (Aug. 15, 1956) erupted with uncharacteristic ardor. "The Roman Catholic Church is not reconciled to those aspects of the Constitution of the United States, and in particular of the First Amendment, which keep Church and State separate, make illegal the use of tax money for the support of religious establishments and insist that all churches shall stand on equal footing in their relation to the State." The journal opposed Wagner and Kennedy because neither "has demonstrated sufficient independence so that he can be trusted to stand against the never ceasing drive of the Roman Catholic Church for access to public funds . . . and for preferential treatment by public figures and bodies."

Kennedy narrowly lost the nomination to Tennessee Senator Estes Kefauver, a sentimental favorite, but enthusiastically campaigned for the ticket. (JFK had placed Stevenson's name in nomination.) Eisenhower received a record Catholic vote for a Republican (49% in Gallup, 53% in the University of Michigan survey), but there is no evidence that failure to nominate Kennedy had anything to do with it. Foreign policy issues and the personal charisma of Eisenhower were the dominant reasons.

The 1958 election was a dress rehearsal for the public raising of the religious issue in 1960. The issue arose primarily in two states, California and Pennsylvania. In California a referendum on tax exemption of parochial school property was the occasion for an outpouring of verbal hostility to Catholicism. Catholic schools were called "unAmerican" in the literature of the forces promoting "Proposition 16," to deny tax exemption. The usual anti-Catholic smears were prominent. I personally examined the materials on file at the Fair Campaign Practices Committee (FCPC) in Washington and it is my conclusion that the Proposition 16 forces were mostly dishonest and unfair in their tactics. They were opposed by many church-state separationists and political and religious liberals, including Episcopal Bishop James Pike. Lutherans, Seventh-day Adventists, and Episcopalians opposed the measure. It was decisively rejected.

During the same election California Attorney General Edmund Brown, the Democratic gubernatorial nominee and a Roman Catholic, was denounced by fundamentalists because he had ruled against obligatory Bible-reading in public schools. The old canards about Catholic hatred of the Bible were bandied about in some of the extremist religious press. Since Brown defeated his Republican opponent, Senator William Knowland, by a 60%–40% vote landslide, the religious issue certainly must not have hurt him substantially. He won the Protestant Central Valley as well as the urban Catholic and Jewish areas.

In Pennsylvania, however, Pittsburgh Mayor David Lawrence's Catholicism almost cost him the election for governor. A widely respected Stevensonian liberal, Lawrence was heavily favored to defeat a Republican nonentity, businessman Arthur McGonigle, who had never held public office. Pennsylvania had never had a Catholic governor, and the rural Protestant Bible Belt reacted with a vengeance. Though Lawrence won, by fewer than 100,000 votes out of almost 4 million cast, his victory came from the Catholic, Jewish, and more liberal Protestant urban and suburban areas. Lawrence ran poorly in the Protestant strongholds which had buried Al Smith under an avalanche in 1928. Lawrence ran way behind the incumbent Democratic Governor George Leader, a chicken farmer by occupation and his party's candidate for U.S. Senator. Though Lawrence won and Leader lost to popular liberal Republican Congressman Hugh Scott,

Lawrence ran badly in the Bible Belt.

The FCPC, in a September 1959 memorandum, concluded that there had been a shocking increase in anti-Catholicism in the 1958 election. The FCPC was organized in 1954 to fight political chicanery and dishonest campaign tactics. It was, under the leadership of executive director Bruce L. Felknor and chairman Charles P. Taft, especially sensitive to religious and racial smears.

Despite the escalating bias, 5 new Catholic governors and 8 new U.S. senators were elected in the 1958 Democratic sweep.

The Louisiana governor's race in January 1960 showed that even in a strongly Catholic state Protestant hostility could still block a Catholic candidate's chances.

DeLesseps Morrison, the suave, liberal mayor of New Orleans, was defeated in a bitter, close race by Jimmy Davis, a semiliterate racist whose only claim to fame was having written the country music hit "You Are My Sunshine" (which propelled him into the governor's chair in the 1940's). The religious/political cleavage was complete. Every Protestant parish went for Davis; almost every Catholic one for Morrison. There were Protestants, of course, who favored Morrison and Catholic racists in Plaquemines parish who went for Davis, but local observers attributed the outcome to the religious factor.

Blacks—Protestants and Catholics—favored Morrison overwhelmingly but thousands of potential black voters, especially in the Protestant parishes, were prohibited from registering to vote by the local segregationist establishment. An American Jewish Committee survey found that Baptist parishes were much more likely to prohibit blacks from voting than the somewhat more tolerant Catholic parishes.[8]

A *New York Times* poll reported that 70% of the North

Louisiana Protestants would not vote for a Catholic governor.[9] It wasn't until the 1970's that a French Catholic, Edwin W. Edwards, could be elected Louisiana's governor, though many Catholics had been elected to Congress.

6

The John F. Kennedy Campaign

Senator John F. Kennedy decided to seek the Presidency at least by 1959. His landslide reelection to the Senate and his expanding record as a spokesman for liberal, progressive causes made him a strong possibility. He was quite different from Al Smith in almost every respect. He had been schooled almost exclusively in non-Catholic private schools. He was a Harvard University graduate and an avid student of history. His *Profiles in Courage*, a biographical study of political integrity, won a Pulitzer Prize. He was literate, urbane, and eloquent.

His legislative record was that of a moderate liberal and he had taken some bold positions on federal aid to education and the independence of Algeria. He understood the important role thrust upon the United States in the international arena and knew instinctively that democracy and liberty had to be made a reality at home before they could be exported.

Kennedy hoped that there would not be a substantial religious question in the 1960 campaign but he soon became aware of the intensity of the issue, even in the quiescent preelection year of 1959. In a *Look* interview (March 3, 1959) Kennedy pledged unequivocal support for the uniquely American principle of church-state separation, opposed public aid for parochial schools, and opposed an ambassador to the Vatican. Most secular journalists and pragmatic politicians applauded the young senator, but, ironically, many Catholics and some moderate Protestants criticized him for sounding too secular. Kennedy had said, "Whatever one's religion in his private life may be, for the officeholder, nothing takes precedence over his oath to uphold the Constitution and all its parts—including the First Amendment and the strict separation of church and state." Patricia Barrett commented, "Some commentators thought Mr. Kennedy had gone too far in asserting the primacy of political over other loyalties and had thus deepened the cleavage between religion and public life."[1] *America,* the distinguished Jesuit weekly, rebuked him (as they were to do again in early 1962): "Our own reaction to the controverted *Look* interview is one of impatience at the earnest Massachusetts Senator's efforts to appease bigots, rather than of disagreement with the positive points he made. A Catholic political candidate, if he must make a profession of his faith, should not seem to give quarter to religious bigotry, even at the risk of having his words distorted. We were somewhat taken aback, for instance, by the unvarnished statement that 'whatever one's religion in his private life . . . nothing takes precedence over his oath. . . .' Mr. Kennedy doesn't really believe that. No religious man, be he Catholic, Protestant or Jew, holds such an opinion."[2]

Lutheran scholar Martin Marty thought that Kennedy was "spiritually rootless and politically almost disturbingly secular." Robert McAfee Brown, a Presbyterian, thought that in Kennedy's " 'effort' to assure his possible constituency that he is just a regular American, he has succeeded only in demonstrating that he is a rather irregular Christian."[3]

Kennedy's forthright advocacy did not convince the unconvinceable. Religious News Service reported in November 1959 that the Texas Baptist convention,

"adopted a resolution cautioning members . . . against
voting for a Roman Catholic candidate," while Alabama
Baptists "went on record as protesting against the election of any Roman Catholic as U.S. President." The National Association of Evangelicals adopted a statement
that read in part, "Any country the Roman Catholic
Church dominates suppresses the right of Evangelicals.
. . . For that reason, thinking Americans view with alarm
the possible election of a Roman Catholic as President of
the United States."[4]

Dr. Ramsey Pollard, president of the Southern Baptist
Convention, announced that he would not "stand by and
keep my mouth shut when a man under control of the
Roman Catholic Church runs for the Presidency of the
United States."[5] Pollard was to open his mouth many
times in 1960, mostly to put his foot in it.

Senator Kennedy did well in the early primaries and
won convincingly in Wisconsin, where a heavy Catholic
Republican crossover contributed to his victory over
Senator Hubert Humphrey of Minnesota. The voting
results showed a Protestant/Catholic division, which
would make the religious issue even more crucial.
Kennedy had to win the primary on May 10 in heavily
Protestant West Virginia if his credibility as a winner was
to be established. He won a decisive 62% landslide, forc-
ing Humphrey's withdrawal. The last real barrier to the
nomination had been met.

Before the West Virginia primary Kennedy addressed
the American Society of Newspaper Editors in Washington on April 21, 1960. He told the four hundred newsmen, "I want no votes solely on account of my religion."
He warned them not to "magnify" or "oversimplify" the
religious issue. "I am not the Catholic candidate for
President. I do not speak for the Catholic Church on
issues of public policy—and no one in that Church
speaks for me." He concluded: "If there is bigotry in the

country so great as to prevent fair consideration of a Catholic who has made clear his complete independence and dedication to the separation of church and state, then we ought to know it. But I do not believe this is the case. I believe the American people are more concerned with a man's views and abilities than with the church to which he belongs. I believe that the founding fathers meant it when they provided in the Constitution that there should be no religious test for office."[6]

Many Protestant leaders endorsed Kennedy's views and commended him publicly. Included were Methodist Bishop G. Bromley Oxnam, Presbyterian Moderator Eugene Carson Blake, Dean Francis B. Sayre of Washington Cathedral, and Dr. Edward Hughes Pruden of Washington's First Baptist Church. Several Methodist, Presbyterian, and Lutheran conclaves rejected resolutions urging defeat of a Catholic candidate.

As Senator Kennedy was being nominated on the first ballot in Los Angeles in July, two significant statements of prominent religious leaders suggested the tenor of the fall campaign. On July 3, Dr. W. A. Criswell delivered a fiery sermon in Dallas' First Baptist Church denouncing "Roman Catholicism's bloody hand" and warning that Kennedy's election would "spell the death of a free church in a free state and our hopes of continuance of full religious liberty in America."[7] Archbishop Karl J. Alter of Cincinnati issued a statement denying that Catholics in America "will use religious toleration here to gain the ascendancy" or "to deprive our fellow citizens of freedom of religion or conscience. . . . We seek no privileged status; we proclaim our full adherence to the provisions of the Constitution as of now as well as for the future."[8] (Unfortunately for Kennedy, the Vatican newspaper *L'Osservatore Romano* in mid-May declared that the Roman Catholic hierarchy had "the right and duty" to advise Roman Catholics how to vote. This editorial was designed for Italy but its timing and tastelessness hurt Kennedy's chances.)

The religious issue smoldered in late summer and started burning by September. Bruce Felknor of the FCPC warned on August 25 that "the circulation of rabidly anti-Catholic material" led to "a substantial danger that the campaign will be dirtier on the religious issue than it was in 1928."[9]

On September 7 at Washington's fashionable Mayflower Hotel, 150 conservative, evangelical, and fundamentalist Protestants of 37 denominations held a one-day national conference of the so-called Citizens for Religious Freedom. Such notables as Dr. Norman Vincent Peale, of *The Power of Positive Thinking* fame, Dr. Daniel A. Poling, editor of *Christian Herald,* Dr. L. Nelson Bell of *Christianity Today,* and Dr. Harold J. Ockenga, author and theologian, appeared. The group issued a policy statement, denying that it was bigotry to question the credentials of a Roman Catholic candidate. They felt that "it is inconceivable that a Roman Catholic president would not be under extreme pressure by the hierarchy of his church to accede to its policies." The statement drew attention to religious liberty problems in many Catholic countries and alleged canon law restrictions on a Catholic President's attendance at interfaith worship services. It pointed out that Kennedy had favored public aid to parochial schools while in the 81st Congress, though admitting that he was the only Roman Catholic senator to oppose the Morse Amendment, which would have provided partial grants and loans for parochial school construction. They claimed that "the nature of the Roman Catholic Church" created "the religious issue in the present campaign."[10]

On the face of it there were several absurdities, nonsequiturs, and downright faulty reasoning in this group's statement. They denounced religious persecution in

Catholic countries, as if Senator Kennedy should be blamed for these excesses. Why not blame Protestant candidates for anti-Catholic discrimination in Sweden? They drew attention to Ohio, "a state with a Roman Catholic governor," where "nuns may be placed on the public payroll as school teachers according to an attorney general's ruling."

They failed, conveniently, to mention that the Ohio attorney general was a Protestant and that these conditions had occurred under several Protestant governors. This was rank dishonesty.

The statement was immediately denounced by Dr. Harold E. Fey, editor of the *Christian Century* (Sept. 14, 1960), and a critic of Catholicism himself, "It misrepresents the breadth of Protestant interests, the intelligence of Protestant concerns, the charity of Protestant attitudes." Scholars Reinhold Niebuhr and John C. Bennett called it "blind prejudice," and then noted significantly, "Most of those Protestants who have been in the forefront of this effort would oppose any liberal Democrat regardless of his religion."[11] The Niebuhr-Bennett statement has great import. Without question, the Citizens for Religious Freedom were preponderantly Republican and conservative. They had a streak of cultural snobbery, a belief that only WASP's were good Americans, that a Catholic or a Jew, or a slightly offbeat Protestant should not be President. Dr. Peale expressed that view beautifully when he said: "Our American culture is at stake. . . . I don't say it won't survive, but it won't be what it was."[12] Someone should have told the good doctor that America had long since entered a post-Protestant phase, perhaps even a post-Christian one. (Adlai Stevenson is supposed to have quipped in Minneapolis, "I find St. Paul appealing and St. Peale appalling.") Peale was apparently embarrassed by the publicity surrounding his participation in

the conference and he later disassociated himself from
it.

It was apparent to Senator Kennedy and his staff that
he had to make a dramatic declaration of independence
from his church's political involvement in order to allay
the lingering suspicions of many Protestants. He accepted an invitation to address the Ministerial Association of Greater Houston on September 12, 1960. Before
perhaps a thousand ministers and laymen, and thousands more who would watch the event on television,
Kennedy directly confronted the issue and pledged absolute adherence to the U.S. Constitution. He promised
to resign rather than submit to clerical dictation. In
words that will echo through the centuries, he said: "I
believe in an America where the separation of church
and state is absolute—where no Catholic prelate would
tell the President (should he be Catholic) how to act and
no Protestant minister would tell his parishioners for
whom to vote—where no church or church school is
granted any public funds or political preference—and
where no man is denied public office merely because his
religion differs from the President who might appoint
him or the people who might elect him.

"I believe in an America that is officially neither Catholic, Protestant nor Jewish—where no public official either
requests or accepts instructions on public policy from
the Pope, the National Council of Churches, or any other
ecclesiastical source—where no religious body seeks to
impose its will directly or indirectly upon the general
populace or the public acts of its officials—and where
religious liberty is so indivisible that an act against one
church is treated as an act against all."

He reminded the listeners that prejudice against one
faith should be construed as prejudice against all. "For
while this year it may be a Catholic against whom the
finger of suspicion is pointed, in other years it has been,

and may someday be again, a Jew—or a Quaker—or a Unitarian—or a Baptist." Almost emotionally and poignantly he reminded fair-minded Americans that thousands of Catholics and Jews died fighting for the freedom we all enjoy today.

"This is the kind of America I believe in—and this is the kind of America I fought for in the South Pacific and the kind my brother died for in Europe. No one suggested then that we might have a 'divided loyalty,' that we did 'not believe in liberty' or that we belonged to a disloyal group that threatened 'the freedom for which our forefathers died.'

"And in fact this is the kind of America for which our forefathers did die when they fled here to escape religious test oaths, that denied office to members of less favored churches, when they fought for the Constitution, the Bill of Rights, the Virginia Statute of Religious Freedom, and when they fought at the shrine I visited today —the Alamo. For side by side with Bowie and Crockett died Fuentes and McCafferty and Baily and Bedillo and Carey—but no one knows whether they were Catholics or not. For there was no religious test there."[13]

To thunderous applause Kennedy exited the room. The conference was televised again and again during the remaining weeks of the campaign.

Kennedy was reinforced by two important declarations. On September 12, one hundred Protestant, Catholic, Jewish, and Greek Orthodox churchmen and scholars issued a statement deploring the religious issue as a violation of Article VI of the U.S. Constitution that "no religious test shall ever be required as a qualification to any office or public trust under the United States." It denounced "the exclusion of members of any family of faith from public office on the basis of religious affiliation." Episcopal bishops were prominently identified with this declaration. The Presiding Bishop, Right Reverend Arthur C. Lichtenberger, Bishops Horace Donegan of New York, Angus Dun of Washington Cathedral, James Pike of San Francisco, Henry Knox Sherrill, and Dean Francis B. Sayre of Washington Cathedral were among the signers. Methodist Bishop G. Bromley Oxnam, Baptist Dr. Carlyle Marney, and Methodist Dr. Dudley Ward were included.[14]

On October 5, "A Statement on Religious Liberty by American Catholic Laymen," signed by 166 prominent Catholics from every walk of life, was published. It was the clearest defense of religious freedom and separation of church and state ever issued by an American Catholic group. It was widely and deservedly praised.[15]

Other groups seeking to counter the continuing viciousness of religious slander included the American Jewish Committee, the American Jewish Congress, the National Council of Churches, the Anti-Defamation League of B'nai B'rith, which exposed the hate literature, the previously mentioned Fair Campaign Practices Committee, and the National Conference of Christians and Jews.

Unfortunately and not unexpectedly, the unappeasable bigots made a major effort in the campaign's home stretch to defame Kennedy and his faith. Author James Michener, who played a leading role in the Kennedy campaign in Bucks County, Pennsylvania, was sickened and shocked by the flood of anti-Catholic garbage spreading throughout his well-educated and presumably enlightened county. Lurid photos of Protestants being burned and tortured by leering priests filled the mailboxes of residents. One Lutheran minister reportedly warned his congregation that Protestants would be hanged in the town square of Levittown if Kennedy were elected. Michener feared the impact of such irrationality and thought Kennedy might lose the election because of it.[16]

It should be noted in passing that America's intellectual community, its writers and professors, and so forth, strongly favored Kennedy. He received the endorsements of most of the significant journals of opinion: *Harper's, Atlantic, New Republic, New Leader, Nation, Progressive,* etc. Most intellectuals likely shared the judgment of Arthur Schlesinger that Richard Nixon was the "hollow man" of American politics, without principle, substance, or vision. Though their hearts probably belonged to Adlai Stevenson, they agreed with Stevenson that Nixon was a middle-class Joe McCarthy, dangerously unfit to lead America through the uncertain 1960's. To his credit, Nixon denounced the use of religion in the campaign, though he did seem to say in one of the Kennedy-Nixon debates that no atheist could ever be considered a potential President.

Dulce and Richter noted, "The religious issue had 'gone underground' following the repercussions of the Peale controversy and the Houston speech, but it continued to add no less heat to the steadily intensified campaign."[17] Conservative Protestants attempted to make Reformation Sunday, October 30, an occasion for a last-ditch "stop Kennedy" effort. Some Catholic bishops in Puerto Rico at this time called on Catholic voters to oust Governor Muñoz Marín, who supported divorce and birth control. Some Protestants seized on this local hierarchy's decision as "proof" that Kennedy could not disentangle himself from his bishops. Some of the attacks on Kennedy were absurd as well as unfair. One Baptist preacher in St. Louis formed an "unlock" club. His supporters wore buttons showing Baptist churches in Spain padlocked, and said that they would vote against Kennedy unless and until Baptist churches in Spain were reopened.

The FCPC in February 1962 analyzed 1,383 reports of 402 "unfair" anti-Catholic political attacks and 392 pieces of "unfair" anti-Catholic literature. The largest numbers were distributed in California, Pennsylvania, and Minnesota, and the committee estimated that 20 to 25 million pieces of such literature were circulated in the United States. The literature was placed in four categories: vile, 5%; dishonest, 25%; unfair, 35%; and responsible, 35%. Patricia Barrett has written, "Although the volume of printed matter dealing with the religious issue in the 1960 campaign was *substantially greater* [author's emphasis] than in 1928, the quality was, on the whole, higher."[18]

Barrett analyzed the content of the literature on file with the FCPC in Washington. I, too, have personally examined the material (and some additional material in the Americans United archives) and substantially agree with her interpretation. She boils the "essence of the anti-Catholic argument" down to five basic concepts:

1. Roman Catholicism does not accept, on principle, the American system of separation of church and state as embodied in the First Amendment, but abides by it as a matter of expediency. The threat to the liberties of non-Catholics is consequently proportionate to the political power which Catholics achieve, since they are conscience-bound to implement the "established church" doctrine whenever this becomes possible.

2. Catholics have a "dual allegiance," to the Pope in Rome and to the United States, with priority automatically accorded to the former in cases of conflict.

3. The "hierarchy" controls the decision of Catholic laymen in all matters, even those that are strictly political.

4. The immediate aim of the Church in this country is to procure public money for its schools and to enact Catholic morality into civil law on such issues as birth control, marriage, and medical practices.

5. Wealth and moral laxity too often characterize the lives of the Catholic clergy.[19]

In a tense, dramatic election, with a record turnout of 68.3 million voters, John F. Kennedy was narrowly elected. Religion was a major factor in the structure of the vote and, on balance, Kennedy lost more than he gained because of it. Though most of the religious issue was disgraceful, there was a silver lining that Dulce and Richter observed: "The election of a President of Catholic faith in 1960 gave a ringing stamp of recognition to pluralism as an indelible fact of national and political and social life. . . . The religious issue generated healthy discussion regarding the separation of church and state, and also raised questions as to the proper degree and the character of influence exercised by churches in the country's political affairs."[20]

7

Religious Factors in the 1960 Vote

John F. Kennedy narrowly defeated Richard M. Nixon 34.2 to 34.1 million, a dramatic finish to one of the more exciting Presidential elections in American history. Religiously, John F. Kennedy won because of enormous backing from minority groups. Jews gave him 82% of their vote and Catholics 78%. (The University of Michigan survey is even higher, showing a Jewish majority of 88% and a Catholic of 81%.) Black Americans, almost all Protestant, gave the Massachusetts senator 68% to 75%. (Gallup shows 68%; Levy-Kramer, 75%.) Protestants favored Richard Nixon 62% to 38%, only 1% less than Eisenhower's 63% in 1956. Since blacks are included in the Protestant figure, one can assume that Kennedy ran a shade behind Stevenson among white Protestants. Kennedy gained at least 27% among Catholics, 7% among Jews, and 7% to 14% among blacks. He could not have won without a respectable Protestant showing, but his outstanding triumph among Catholics and Jews, who turned out in large numbers, saved the day for him.

Kennedy carried heavily Catholic states such as Massachusetts, Rhode Island, New York, New Jersey, and Connecticut. He also carried states with a virtual absence of Catholics, for example, Alabama, Georgia, North Carolina, South Carolina, and Arkansas. If we take the nation as a whole, though, Kennedy's *gain* over Stevenson's

1956 vote is positively related to the Catholic percentage of the population. In the 10 heaviest Catholic states Kennedy gained 21.4%, but in the 10 least Catholic states he gained only 1%.

Though Catholics went solidly for Kennedy, there were sharp differences in income and education categories. Wealthier, more highly educated Catholics were twice as likely to vote for Nixon as the more modestly educated and poorer Catholics, and 82% of Catholic Republicans still voted for Nixon.

The book from which the above statistics were derived, Mark R. Levy and Michael S. Kramer's superb *The Ethnic Factor,* did not include German Catholics. My research indicates a solid Kennedy majority among German Catholics but one that did not reach the 75% to 85% level. The 15 heaviest German Catholic counties gave Kennedy 58%. Since there are non-Catholics in these counties, Kennedy's Catholic vote may have been 70% or so. In some German Catholic towns and villages, Kennedy did sweep 85% to 90%, though.

Some independent research of mine confirms the Catholic swing to Kennedy. In the 106 heaviest Catholic counties, Kennedy won 62.5%, compared to 41.1% for Stevenson, a 21.4% gain. (In the 15 urban counties, Kennedy won 61%, Stevenson, 41%.) The turnout increase over 1956 was 19%, considerably above the national figure—which undoubtedly helped John F. Kennedy. In the "top 20" Catholic counties, which are almost entirely Catholic enclaves in Texas, Louisiana, and New Mexico, Kennedy swept 70%, compared to Stevenson's 46%, and the turnout increased by a phenomenal 36%. Many new Catholic voters were obviously won by John F. Kennedy.

To see the magnitude of the Catholic swing to Kennedy, we shall take a brief tour through the small towns and villages of the Midwest, where a traditional ambience of Europe prevails. In these little Catholic towns, one feels as if transported to Bavaria, Holland, or Belgium. Pride in a Catholic candidate and resentment at the bitter and unfair attacks on him produced an avalanche in certain communities. Anyone who denies the importance of religion on voting should look at results like these.

In Emmons County, North Dakota, the town of Hague voted 161–26 for Kennedy after going 167–20 for Eisenhower. The village of Lake in the same county went 70–1 for Kennedy, though just four years before they had liked Ike 47–26. Similar results turn up in other Catholic towns. In Doll, North Dakota (Morton County), Kennedy beat Nixon 38–6; Eisenhower beat Stevenson 37–7. In Union Township West, in Putnam County, Ohio, Kennedy crushed Nixon 181–55 but Eisenhower had walloped Stevenson 181–43. In Lac LaBelle, a lovely town in Waukesha County, Wisconsin, Eisenhower had pulverized Stevenson 136–8, but Kennedy thrashed Nixon 133–80.

German Catholic Republicans switched en masse to Kennedy. I selected counties where pro-Kennedy voting was most prominent and searched the precinct returns where available, discovering a fascinating panorama of religious voting. There were 33 precincts in North Dakota, Ohio, Nebraska, Texas, Iowa, Minnesota, Indiana, and Wisconsin, where half or more of the normally Republican voters liked John F. Kennedy. He swept all 33 precincts, while Stevenson had carried only 1. In some areas Kennedy's margin was phenomenal. In Wild Rose, North Dakota, he won 81–2; in Little Badlands, North Dakota, it was 49–2, and in Little Heart, North Dakota, he led 101–9. In Precinct 3 of Cedar County, Nebraska, it was 194–11. In some Iowa precincts, Kennedy won 289–20 in Kniest (Carroll County), 273–20 in Pleasant Valley (Carroll County), and 327–38 in Prairie Creek (Dubuque County). Kennedy's number one precinct in the entire nation was Sharon, a Polish Catholic agricultural town, in Portage County, Wisconsin, where he won 580–7. (See Appendix, Table 6.)

In Wisconsin, the mosaic of America is at its brightest. In the same or contiguous counties one can find towns that are variously Dutch Catholic, German Lutheran, Belgian Catholic, Norwegian Lutheran, Polish Catholic, Swiss Protestant, and German Reformed, with Moravians and Methodists thrown in for good measure. Episcopalians are staunchly High Church, this being "the biretta belt." There are Jews in Milwaukee and liberal humanist intellectuals in Madison. All in all a political analyst's dream world.

Wisconsin Catholics went heavily for John F. Kennedy, especially in the April primary against Hubert Humphrey. The 11 heaviest Catholic counties gave him 67.9%, and 6 of them gave him over 70%. By contrast the 8 least Catholic counties gave him only 31%, 5 of them giving him less than 30%. Lutheran counties generally went for Humphrey, especially the Scandinavian ones, but Kennedy did well in German Lutheran areas and better in Lutheran counties than in "other Protestant" ones. The religious factor showed up again in the general election, though not as prominently since many German Catholics remained Republican and Scandinavian Lutherans remained Democratic.

There were 120 precincts where Kennedy made impressive gains, carrying 106 of them. Stevenson had carried only 3. In Pepin County's town of Lima, for example, Kennedy won 292–25 compared to Stevenson's 147–111. Kennedy ran 46% ahead of Stevenson in the top ten swing towns, sweeping 69.6% compared to only 23.3%. He ran 9% better than Protestant Democrat Gaylord Nelson (the party's candidate for governor). Slightly greater gains for Kennedy came in Republican Catholic precincts, though his biggest margins were in 10 Polish Democratic precincts in Milwaukee, where he won 89%.

The net gain for Kennedy was about 12 or 12.1 million votes in Catholic America. However, he lost as much as 13.6 million votes among Protestants. A Gallup poll in 1960 showed 20% of the electorate would reject "a generally well qualified Catholic candidate" of either party. Thus, about *26* million of the *68* million Presidential votes were decided by the religious issue. Let us look at the Protestant vote.

Protestants voted 62%–38% for Nixon, according to the Gallup postelection surveys, a gain of only 1% over Stevenson. The University of Michigan survey showed almost identical results. Though Kennedy ran an eyelash ahead of Stevenson, he should have run much better if party affiliation and normal Congressional votes are considered. It is here that Kennedy's slippage is considered to have occurred. Despite some survey data showing a widespread anti-Catholicism in the South, Kennedy ran best (47%) among southern Protestants and worst (28%) among northeastern Protestants. This was certainly due to traditional party preferences. He also ran well among Protestant males, union members, younger voters, and farmers.

The University of Michigan's Survey Research Center found that, on balance, Kennedy lost 1.5 million votes because of his religion. His Catholic gains were slightly offset by Protestant defections. Their researchers discovered that the higher the regularity of church attendance, the higher the anti-Catholic vote. Close to 20% of the Protestants "switched," with those who seldom or never attended church generally switching from Eisenhower to Kennedy while the regular churchgoers shifted from Stevenson to Nixon. Defections were slightly higher (4% to 7%) in the South. (See Phillip E. Converse, *Religion and Politics: The 1960 Elections.*)

To test these findings, I looked at the 1956 and 1960 vote in heavily Baptist, Lutheran, Methodist, and Mormon counties to see if anti-Catholic voting was widespread. Then, to look at the opposite side of the coin, I listed the counties where the heaviest anti-Kennedy voting was found and checked the religious identification to see if any common patterns emerge.

Anti-Catholic voting was widespread in the border states, particularly in rural Missouri, Oklahoma, Kentucky, Tennessee, central Pennsylvania, and the Central Valley of California. In the Deep South, it is difficult to measure anti-Catholic voting because of racial animosities, northern emigration, and the existence of state's rights third parties on the ballot in 1956 and 1960 in Louisiana, Mississippi, Arkansas, Tennessee, South Carolina, and Virginia.

There are 45 counties in a dozen states where anti-Catholic voting was considerable. Stevenson carried 32 of the counties but Kennedy only 15. Some of the heaviest anti-Catholic voting appeared in southeast Missouri and northeast Arkansas, where Kennedy ran about 15% behind Stevenson. Catholics are poorly represented in these 45 counties. In only one county (Roosevelt, New Mexico) are they found in proportion to their national figure and even here many are recent migrants. Baptists are the leading faith in 33 counties, Lutherans or Methodists in 12. In some counties John Kennedy ran *worse* than Al Smith; in several counties he was the first Democrat in history to lose, for example, Dunklin County in Missouri and Dyer and Madison Counties in Tennessee. The fact that an anti-trend of 10% to 15% against Kennedy was found in so many counties indicates the thrust and persistence of anti-Catholicism in rural America.

Focusing on certain precincts shows some stunning anti-Catholic voting. In the hamlet of Arch, New Mexico,

Stevenson beat Eisenhower 40–23, but Nixon crushed Kennedy 71–20. More than 4 of every 10 voters switched to Nixon in this Baptist community in Roosevelt County. In Perry, Kennedy was wiped out 12–0, though Stevenson had received 5 votes in 1956. In nearby Dora, Stevenson's 147–121 margin became a whopping 195–80 for Nixon. In McCracken County, Kentucky, Kennedy lost Milan 103–45, but Stevenson had carried it 105–61. Similarly, in Houckamp, Stevenson's 638–137 landslide declined to only 310–254 for Kennedy. In central Pennsylvania, Kennedy lost ground in Protestant rural areas, losing half or more of Stevenson's vote in some communities. In Franklin (Columbia County), Stevenson narrowly lost 81–75, but Kennedy was crushed 148–46. In Huntingdon County's Clay Township, Stevenson won 94–88, but Kennedy lost 145–56. (See Appendix, Table 7.)

In Wisconsin there were 77 precincts where Kennedy ran 10% or more behind Stevenson. Stevenson carried 54 of them; Kennedy, only 19. In 10 precincts Kennedy lost one fifth to one fourth of the Stevenson vote, declining 21.3%. He also ran 14% behind the Protestant Democratic gubernatorial nominee Gaylord Nelson. In Stettin, Precinct 1 (Marathon County), Stevenson had won 139–136; Kennedy lost 235–78. One fourth of the town's voters switched on the religious issue. In Norwegian Lutheran Christiana (Dane County), Kennedy still won, but only by 243–195, compared to Stevenson's 341–104 triumph. In several Swiss Protestant towns in Green County, for example, Monroe and York, Kennedy ran about 20% behind Stevenson.

Two significant facts stand out in this analysis of the religious vote in 1960. One is that the pro-Catholic swing in these counties and precincts exceeded the anti-Catholic. Kennedy often gained 40% to 75% but lost 20% to 40%. The other is the intense discord *within* heavily

Catholic or Protestant counties. Even in counties characterized by enormous pro-Kennedy swings, there were
precincts that went heavily the other way. Perhaps these
were strongholds of the Protestant minority, acting in a
beleaguered way. In evenly divided counties, religious
voting was often very severe, indicating the likelihood of
a rivalry factor. In Kentucky's Nelson and Marion counties, for example, the majority of the population are
Catholics of German descent, but a large and growing
minority are Baptists. In a sample of Catholic strongholds, Kennedy won 88%, but in Baptist areas, he won
only 33%.

Looking at the election from a different perspective
suggests that, though anti-Catholic voting seemed most
vivid in Baptist and Lutheran counties, it was not universally widespread. A study of the 96 heaviest Southern
Baptist counties in Alabama, Florida, Georgia, Kentucky,
Louisiana, Mississippi, North Carolina, Oklahoma,
South Carolina, Tennessee, and Texas shows that
Kennedy ran a little behind Stevenson, polling 47.6%
compared to 49.9%. Ten of the counties shifted allegiance, 7 shifting from Stevenson to Nixon, and 3 from
Eisenhower to Kennedy. It was a relatively poor showing
for Kennedy but not a devastating one.

In the nation's 34 strongest Lutheran counties in Iowa,
Minnesota, Nebraska, North Dakota, South Dakota, and
Wisconsin, Kennedy polled 42.8% and Stevenson 41.
5%.

Methodist counties in Maryland, Delaware, West Virginia, and Kansas, which had rejected Al Smith overwhelmingly, gave Kennedy a respectable vote, several
percentage points better than Stevenson. He also did
considerably better than Stevenson in Mormon bailiwicks in Utah and Idaho.

Jews were strongly loyal to the liberal Democratic heritage and preferred Kennedy solidly over Nixon. The

Levy-Kramer study, based on precinct returns, shows 82% for Kennedy compared to 88% in the University of Michigan survey and 81% by Roper. There were considerable variances. Kennedy won over 90% in Jewish precincts in Brooklyn and Los Angeles, but only 45% to 49% in Cincinnati and the Boston suburbs, where Jewish Republicanism has a long history. He ran at least 7% better than Stevenson, who had been immensely popular among culture-loving, education-respecting Jews, almost everywhere except in the Orthodox Jewish ward in Boston's Mattapan District and an assembly district in Brooklyn, where he ran 1% behind Stevenson.

Jewish organizations were prominent in defending Kennedy from the rabid attacks of fundamentalist bigots. Jews knew that they were only slightly less hated among these groups than Catholics. Election of a Catholic President might also one day lead to the election of a Jew.

8

Religion and Politics Since 1961

Since the Kennedy campaign, the religious issue in national politics has been muted. Until the 1976 election, little if any interest in a candidate's religious affiliation has been noted. The shock of Kennedy's death, at a time when considerable affection for him among Protestant voters was growing, almost buried religious prejudice. I say "almost," because a 1969 Gallup poll revealed that 8% of the electorate would still not vote for a well-qualified Catholic or Jewish Presidential candidate.

One unexpected development has been the quasi-institutionalization of a Catholic as vice-presidential nominee. William E. Miller, Barry Goldwater's 1964 running mate, was a Catholic, as were Democrats Edmund S. Muskie in 1968 and R. Sargent Shriver, Jr., in 1972. Almost no objection was made toward Miller, even among the fundamentalist lunatic fringe, though some Tennessee Republican delegates demurred at his selection. In 1968, the two leading nonestablishment Democrats, Robert Kennedy and Eugene McCarthy, were Roman Catholics, but no serious objections were raised.

In 1964, Republican Barry Goldwater inherited a rather curious alliance of fundamentalist Protestants and conservative Roman Catholics. Goldwater and the Republican platform urged passage of a prayer amendment, which solidified their support among many fundamentalists. Martin Marty, in his *A Nation of Behavers* (The University of Chicago Press, 1976), claims that the Goldwater nomination was "the high-tide" of the resurgence of fundamentalists and neo-evangelicals in American politics. Erling Jorstad, in his *The Politics of Doomsday*, says emphatically, "The Fundamentalists of the far right had consciously and enthusiastically involved themselves for the first time in a national campaign." The *New York Times* (Aug. 9, 1964) reported that Billy James Hargis had proclaimed that Goldwater's election "would be the millennium."

Many Roman Catholic voters responded favorably to Goldwater's appeal. He ran 2% better than Nixon among all Catholic voters, but ran as much as 15% better in Slavic Catholic neighborhoods in Baltimore and Gary and in Italian Catholic South Philadelphia. He carried a German Catholic precinct in Sturgeon Bay, Wisconsin, which had gone for Kennedy. Of the 5 counties outside of the South which switched from Kennedy to Goldwater, 2 were German Catholic—Emmons County, North Dakota, and Osage County, Missouri; 2 were Mormon counties in Idaho; and 1 was a Methodist stronghold in Maryland.

In local politics religious bias appears in isolated instances. In Oklahoma's 1966 governor's race, a Roman Catholic Republican, Dewey Bartlett, though successful, ran a little behind Barry Goldwater, who lost Oklahoma in 1964, in a few counties where anti-Kennedy voting was notable. In New Mexico considerable anti-Catholic voting was apparent in the 1966 governor's race in several Baptist strongholds in east New Mexico's Little Dixie area. Again a Catholic Republican, David Cargo, lost votes that had gone to Barry Goldwater and Richard Nixon. In 9 southern Protestant counties, Cargo ran 1% behind Goldwater and 11% behind Nixon. (Kennedy ran 3% behind Stevenson.) In some counties, for example,

Roosevelt, the anti-Catholic vote was large. In the Hispanic Catholic counties, Kennedy ran 14% better than Stevenson, and Cargo ran 15% ahead of Goldwater.

In general, though, religious influences on politics have become more sophisticated and issue-oriented. Since Kennedy's carefully delineated posture on church-state relations, most candidates since 1964 have dealt with and spelled out their views, knowing that at least some voters will take them into consideration.

RELIGION IN THE 1972 CAMPAIGN

The 1972 Presidential campaign was suffused with more religious issues than any national campaign since 1960. Throughout much of the campaign, the national press emphasized the attempts to sway Catholic and Jewish voters away from their historic Democratic leaning to the Republicans as part of President Nixon's "New American Majority." Early surveys indicated that Catholic voters gave 53% to 56% of their vote to Nixon, thereby supporting a Republican Presidential candidate for the first time in history.

Nixon adviser and political strategist Kevin Phillips, in his 1969 book *The Emerging Republican Majority,* postulated that Catholic voters were ready to embrace a more Republican and conservative political philosophy, and that they would become a logical element in a new Republican coalition. A growing social conservatism among Catholic voters was regarded as the reason for the disenchantment with the more liberal Democratic Party. NBC estimated that 56% of the national Catholic vote went to Nixon, compared to 33% in 1968. In certain areas the swing was even heavier over the same span. In an Irish Catholic area of Queens, New York, Nixon increased his vote from 17% to 68%. In Italian Catholic areas of New York State, Nixon increased the vote from

51% to 68%, in New Jersey from 41% to 61%, and in Massachusetts from 18% to 36%. In heavily Polish Catholic Ward 2 of Baltimore, Nixon polled 63% compared to 23% in 1968. Two assembly districts in Queens gave Nixon 80% of the Catholic vote, while Italian Catholic neighborhoods in Bay Ridge, Brooklyn, gave the President 77%.

During his Presidency, Nixon made direct appeals to partisan Catholic interests. In a 1969 speech on Vietnam he specifically singled out the alleged 1.5 million Catholic refugees from North Vietnam as one of the reasons for his refusal to abandon South Vietnam. In addition to his appointment of Henry Cabot Lodge as his personal emissary to the Vatican, Nixon's 1971 statement on abortion indicated strong support for a specifically Catholic position on that issue. In his statement, Nixon reversed the Department of Defense decision to liberalize the abortion regulations in mainland military hospitals. The President ordered each military base to follow the generally restrictive laws in the state in which it was located. The President denounced abortion as an "unacceptable form of population control which I cannot square with my personal belief in the sanctity of human life," ignoring the fact that individual decisions about terminating problem pregnancies are not made with population control in mind. The President continued this strict antiabortion policy in a 1971 letter which he sent to Terence Cardinal Cooke, in which he clearly identified himself with the hierarchy's effort to repeal the liberal abortion law in New York State. The political effect in New York State was calculated to solidify the conservative Catholic bloc for the President.

The President's strongest identification with specific Catholic interests had been his endorsement of public aid for parochial schools. The President's pro-parochiaid speeches to the Knights of Columbus in 1971 and before the National Catholic Educational Association in 1972 thrust this sectarian issue into the Presidential campaign. The 1972 Republican platform, like the Republican platform of 1968, endorsed aid to parochial schools. Indeed, the 1968 Republican platform was more positive in its approach to parochiaid than the Democratic. Bishop William McManus of Chicago reminded the Democrats at the 1972 platform hearings in Miami that the favorable 1968 platform of the Republicans may have been a contributing factor in the swing to Nixon among many Catholic voters in 1968. Throughout the campaign the President repeated his support for a tax-credit scheme to aid parochial schools. In late October, during a major radio address, he repeated his "unequivocal and irrevocable support" for the tax-credit parochiaid proposal.

The 1972 Democratic platform committed the party to "channel financial aid by a constitutional formula to children in nonpublic schools." Senator George McGovern, who had previously opposed parochiaid as unconstitutional, capitulated in an attempt to blunt Nixon's edge on this issue. Speaking in Chicago at a Catholic high school in September, McGovern endorsed the concept of federal aid to parochial education. His running mate, Sargent Shriver, whose Catholicism was undoubtedly a factor in his being chosen as vice-presidential nominee, went even farther. In a September speech at Loras College in Dubuque, Iowa, Shriver strongly endorsed government aid to parochial schools and promised to find some way to help them.

One additional aspect that needs comment was noted by *Washington Star-News* columnist Milton Viorst: "In 1972 it is clear that Senator George McGovern was determined to have a Catholic running with him. In selecting Eagleton and Shriver the Democrats have almost institutionalized the presence of a Catholic on the ticket.

It is now likely that in the future, Democrats will offer a balanced ticket of 1 Protestant, 1 Catholic."[1]

On the practical level, both political parties exploited religious issues considerably during the Presidential campaign. Prominent ads were placed by the Committee to Re-elect the President (CREEP) in Catholic diocesan newspapers in mid-October. Nixon's aid virtually promised that the President would save parochial schools in the United States and accused Senator McGovern of insufficient support for these schools. CREEP also established a so-called heritage division which was charged with appealing primarily to the various ethnic communities in the United States, most of them Roman Catholic. This well-funded division got the President's message across to millions of ethnic voters who cast their first Republican Presidential ballot. The Democratic Party also reactivated its nationalities division and formed various "Catholics for McGovern" committees in different states. Their lack of funds, however, and the timing of their formation prevented them from holding more of the Catholic vote for the Democrats. Senator McGovern also placed some ads in Catholic diocesan newspapers, but they did not play up the religious issue, though one ad did show Senator McGovern being greeted by the late Pope John in 1962, when McGovern was director of President Kennedy's Food for Peace Program.

On the local level, distinctly sectarian appeals were generally confined to areas where aid to parochial schools has become a divisive local issue. This was particularly true in Pennsylvania, where ads placed in both diocesan and general newspapers pledged support for Catholic schools. Msgr. William Novicky, superintendent of the Cleveland Catholic schools, on September 20 urged Catholic parents not to vote for any political candidates without first checking to see whether the candidate favored aid to parochial schools. The abortion issue figured prominently in two referenda and also in New York State politics. In the 85th assembly district of New York (The Bronx), leaflets depicting dead fetuses attacked the Democratic candidate, Anthony Mercurella, calling the Catholic Democrat a murderer for having voted against abortion repeal in Albany.

Another interesting aspect of the campaign was the rather large number of religious leaders of many faiths who endorsed Presidential candidates. Religious Leaders for McGovern-Shriver had the support of a large number of clergy of all faiths. Roman Catholic Auxiliary Bishop Thomas Gumbleton of Detroit endorsed Senator McGovern on October 20. Reportedly, Bishop Gumbleton is the first U.S. Catholic prelate to endorse a Presidential candidate since Archbishop John Ireland endorsed William McKinley in 1896. Among the prominent religious leaders endorsing McGovern were Methodist Bishop James Armstrong, theologians John C. Bennett, Robert McAfee Brown, William Sloane Coffin, Harvey Cox, and black evangelist Thomas Skinner, founder of Evangelicals for McGovern.

On the Nixon side, Boston evangelical leader Dr. Harold J. Ockenga and famed evangelist Dr. Billy Graham endorsed the President's reelection. A number of distinguished clergymen who supported President Nixon were invited to the White House on November 2 for briefing. In addition, John Cardinal Krol's appearance at the Republican National Convention was taken as a sign of his implicit support for the President.

Some voters, however, resisted the blandishments of the Nixon campaign and moved in the opposite direction. McGovern made some extraordinary gains in counties containing universities and colleges. He carried Washtenaw County, Michigan, Jackson County, Illinois, and Athens County, Ohio, all of which contain colleges and had supported Nixon twice before. Of the 160 counties where McGovern ran ahead of Humphrey, 13 are heavily college-oriented. Sixteen counties went for Nixon in 1968 and McGovern in 1972. McGovern topped Humphrey by 14% in Amherst, Massachusetts, and carried Durham and Hanover, New Hampshire (college towns that Humphrey had not carried). He ran 8% better than Humphrey in Boston's fashionable, intellectual Beacon Hill Ward 5. He ran 4% ahead of Humphrey in Philadelphia's Ward 5 and 6% better in Ward 27, which contain university and upper-class intelligentsia. McGovern ran ahead of Humphrey in many precincts containing young and well-educated voters in Washington, D.C., and captured 62% in ultrafashionable Georgetown. He swept 78% in 11 student precincts of Madison, Wisconsin, compared to Humphrey's 67%, and, significantly, he received 9,400 more votes than Humphrey, while Nixon picked up only 1,200 new votes. Another stunning gain of 16% for McGovern came in the Aspen, Colorado, ski-resort area.

As for the religious aspect, some fascinating facts turn up in the pro-McGovern swing. In many German and Scandinavian Lutheran and Dutch Protestant counties in the upper Midwest, McGovern topped Humphrey. This is the heartland of isolationist-populist sentiment, which gave Bob La Follette a solid 1924 victory and Wendell Wilkie a 1940 landslide. Anti-war sentiment was strong and many voters opposed Humphrey because of their opposition to the Vietnam war. When Nixon failed to end the war, many independent-minded voters switched to McGovern, "the Prairie Populist." There have also been suggestions that the "morality" vote among staid, sober Midwestern Protestants (and many Catholics) hurt Nixon. These voters early on perceived corruption in the Nixon Administration and responded favorably to George McGovern's moralistic fervor.

Many German Catholics, the most Republican of Catholic ethnic groups, shifted to McGovern for the same reason. Though he ran about 2% behind Humphrey among all German Catholics, McGovern made dramatic and impressive gains in certain precincts of Wisconsin. In fact, of Wisconsin's 15 pro-McGovern trending counties, 6 are Roman Catholic, 5 Lutheran, and 4 divided between Catholic and Lutheran. There were 11 Catholic precincts in 8 Wisconsin counties that switched from Nixon to McGovern in 1972. In 7 of them McGovern gained over 10 percentage points! In De Pere (Brown County), McGovern more than doubled Humphrey's vote. In Calumet County's Brothertown and in Precinct 1 of Durand (Pepin County), McGovern won where Humphrey had lost badly.

In several strong Protestant precincts McGovern gained 13% to 15%. He lost Birnamwood (Shawano County) only 82–75, while Humphrey lost 83–40. Even in a few staunchly Republican precincts McGovern gained 6% to 8%. In the strongly Protestant city of Neenah in Winnebago County, there was a small whittling away of Nixon's strength. Kennedy won 30%, Humphrey 33%, and McGovern 35%.

We can't leave Wisconsin Catholics without a brief mention of another little-known fact. John Schmitz, a Roman Catholic from California's right-wing Orange County, ran for President on the American Party ticket and polled over 1 million votes. His highest percentages came from several Mormon counties in Idaho, rural eastern Oregon, and a few French Catholic parishes in South Louisiana. Upon marinating myself in the Wisconsin election data (as Richard Scammon urges all election buffs to do), I discovered an unusually large Schmitz vote in German Catholic towns and villages. Since no analyses of the Schmitz campaign or vote have been published, I am at a loss to know why. Perhaps his strength was a hangover from Father Coughlin and Joe McCarthy days, when many Catholics found ultraconservative causes appealing. Schmitz won 25% in Auburndale (Wood County), just a shade behind McGovern. He won almost 20% in four other Wood County towns (Lincoln, Marshfield, Auburndale Village, and Cameron).

THE RELIGIOUS FACTOR
IN THE 1974 ELECTIONS

Religious issues played a very limited role in the 1974 Congressional and state house elections. Other than the parochiaid referendum in Maryland and college aid referenda in Massachusetts and Virginia, there were only a few instances in which religion-based issues were involved in the elections. This differs from the strongly religious-influenced Presidential election of 1972.

The use of a candidate's religion as a political issue is rare today. In New York, defeated incumbent Governor Malcolm Wilson's campaign ads mentioned that he was "a deeply religious man." In Maryland's Montgomery County, incumbent county executive James P. Gleason placed large ads in Catholic papers with lists of "distinguished and prominent Catholic lay leaders, Democrats, Independents and Republicans, who endorsed Mr. Gleason." A number of other candidates placed ads in the Washington, D.C. *Catholic Standard*, quietly pointing out to voters that they were members of certain Catholic parishes or had worked for specifically Catholic issues. In Wisconsin's 8th Congressional District, incumbent Representative Harold Froehlich faced an unusual situation in that his Democratic opponent, Robert Cornell, was a Roman Catholic priest. Froehlich had defeated Cornell once before, but this time he was apparently concerned. He asked a Catholic Republican Congressman, Edward J. Derwinski of Illinois, to campaign for him. Derwinski's brother is a monk who once served in the district and was well known there. However, in spite of Froehlich's campaign tactics, Cornell won handily.

The use of religious slander in campaigns has virtually disappeared. Samuel J. Archibald, executive director of the Fair Campaign Practices Committee in Washington, D.C., told me that this was the first campaign in which there were no complaints filed under the subject of religion. This differs from 1970, when 3% of the complaints filed were on religious grounds, and from 1966, when 6% of the complaints were religion-based.

The abortion law issue came up in a number of elections. The national antiabortion groups, working primarily through Catholic dioceses around the country, often endorsed candidates who had pledged to amend the Constitution to deny freedom of choice with regard to abortion. These groups also used questionnaires throughout the country to determine candidate responses. Sample ballots listing antiabortion candidates were distributed in a number of Catholic churches in Maryland. Their threats of intimidation, however, were not credited with much success.

A study by the Planned Parenthood Federation of America revealed that 18 of the 79 House members who were most militantly in favor of an anti freedom of choice on abortion constitutional amendment were defeated, compared to only one of the 38 members who have led the fight against an amendment. An analysis by the National Abortion Rights Action League showed that 41 Congressional opponents of freedom of choice were not reelected, compared to only four defenders of the Supreme Court decision. A number of candidates tried to use the abortion issue to win votes. Among them was Republican Governor Malcolm Wilson of New York, who endorsed the antiabortion amendment and noted this prominently in his campaign literature. He also denounced his successful Democratic opponent, Repre-

sentative Hugh Carey, for refusing to sign the Hogan
antiabortion amendment discharge petition in the last
session of Congress.

In Pennsylvania, opponents of freedom of choice tried
to defeat Governor Milton Shapp, who had vetoed an
abortion restriction bill in 1974. Cardinal Krol and the
Philadelphia *Catholic Standard and Times* attacked the governor in especially harsh terms. A Roman Catholic
bishop from western Pennsylvania intimated that Catholics should bloc-vote against Shapp because of his abortion position. The issue apparently was of minor significance to the electorate since Shapp was easily reelected.
In South Philadelphia's heavily Catholic areas, Governor
Shapp experienced no particular difficulty. He won 69%
of the May primary vote in these Catholic strongholds
against State Representative Martin Mullen, the super-
defender of Catholic interests in Harrisburg, even carrying Mullen's own ward. In the November elections, Governor Shapp carried all but one of these 17 wards and
polled 59% of the vote in them.

In one race the abortion issue is credited with influenc-
ing the outcome. In the Kansas race for U.S. Senate,
Representative William Roy, a Democrat, charged on
NBC-TV election night that the abortion issue was responsible for his narrow defeat by Senator Robert Dole.
Roy charged that the state had been flooded with vicious
antiabortion material during the weekend before the
election, aimed at him because of his admission that he
had performed a number of therapeutic abortions in
order to save the lives of women. Dr. Roy, an obstetrician
from Topeka, had also delivered 5,000 babies, but his
admission that he had performed abortion apparently
cost him votes. ABC-TV reported that a bingo referendum brought out an unusually large Catholic vote in
Topeka, where Roy ran far worse than expected. The
New York Times reported that Senator Dole used the abor-

tion issue frequently in the late days of the campaign by denouncing his opponent as a pro-abortionist and by promising to support "pro-life legislation."

The possibility of a government prayer amendment in Congress surfaced in a few elections. In Florida, Republican Jack Eckerd strongly favored what he called a "return to voluntary prayer in schools," while his opponent, Democrat Richard Stone, did not favor such an amendment. Stone was the winner. In New York State, the gubernatorial candidate of the Courage Party, Dr. Wayne S. Amato, viciously attacked the Supreme Court for allegedly "removing God from our schools." He said the public schools teach "atheism, evolution, and other myths" and called for government prayer amendments. He pulled less than 1% of the vote. *The Wanderer,* an ultraconservative Catholic weekly with nationwide readership, attacked Kansas Representative William Roy, a Methodist, for having voted against the government prayer amendment in 1971.

New York Governor Malcolm Wilson endorsed a prayer amendment in his campaign literature and denounced his opponent Representative Hugh Carey, for voting against the 1971 government prayer amendment. Wilson, in fact, injected so many religious issues into the New York campaign that Carey complained, "I hope this campaign is not going to be decided on who genuflects the most times." Both Wilson and Carey were Roman Catholics. Carey became the first Catholic governor of New York since Al Smith.

A gambling issue brought out a large vote in New Jersey. The proposal to establish casinos in Atlantic City was sent down to a crushing 61%–39% defeat. Religious leaders of all faiths were prominent in defeating this proposal. Perhaps the most bizarre referendum was in Rush Springs, Oklahoma, a tiny community of 1,000

people, which voted to ban both public and private danc-
ing.

It is difficult to know why religious issues did not influence the results as much as in previous years. It may be
that the tensions of the economy, the aftermath of a
Presidential resignation, or the hosts of other problems
appeared more important to the electorate than parochiaid, abortion, or prayer amendments. It is unlikely,
however, that these important issues will go away. Congress and the state legislatures will still have to deal with
them during the coming decade.

THE 1976 CAMPAIGN

The 1976 election saw a return to the intense discussion of religion in politics that characterized the Smith
and Kennedy campaigns. The candidates rather freely
discussed their religious views and values and their
stands on church-state issues. The Democratic liberals
Birch Bayh, Fred Harris, Sargent Shriver, and Morris
Udall took the conventional liberal positions against
government prayer amendments, parochiaid, and antiabortion amendments. In January, Roman Catholic
Shriver issued perhaps the strongest pro-separation
statement of all the candidates: "I believe strongly in the
Constitutional principle of separating church and state.
Our founders were right in fearing that religious freedom would be threatened in the long run by a departure
from governmental neutrality in spiritual matters. So I
support the Supreme Court's decisions limiting public
aid to parochial schools. Direct public aid targeted at
church-related schools, or administered by church officials, would seriously threaten the independence of religion and the First Amendment separation of Church and
State."[2]

Arizona's Morris Udall made a remarkable admission

for an American politician when he announced in January that he "no longer felt the need for institutional religion."[3] Udall broke with his Mormon faith over the issue of excluding blacks from the priesthood, though he was unfairly haunted by his Mormon background during the campaign. Detroit's black Catholic mayor Coleman A. Young, a Jimmy Carter supporter, used the Mormon issue against Udall in the Michigan primary. Later he apologized for misrepresenting Udall's position and Udall gracefully accepted the apology.

The Republican contenders Gerald Ford and Ronald Reagan differed considerably from the Democrats on church-state issues. President Ford has long been an advocate of aid to parochial schools, particularly through the tax credit device. In a 1975 press conference, he indicated his belief that private and parochial education are essential to the nation and should be aided in any way constitutionally possible. He was a major sponsor of the Nixon Administration's tax credit proposals of 1970 and 1971.

While in Congress, Ford voted for the 1971 Wylie Amendment which would have mandated religious exercises in public schools. Ford told a press conference in Durham, New Hampshire, on February 9, 1976, that he supports a prayer amendment. He called the 1962-63 Supreme Court decisions "most unfortunate" and "regrettable."

President Ford, in an attempt to take a "moderate" position, has endorsed a "states' rights" antiabortion amendment to the Constitution. He also admitted voting against a liberalized Michigan abortion law in a 1972 referendum.

Ronald Reagan took the militant antiabortion tack, "repenting" of his "mistake" in signing a liberalized abortion law while governor of California in 1967. He endorsed the Buckley antiabortion amendment, though suggesting safeguards to protect the life of the mother. He tended to favor tax credit and voucher plans to aid nonpublic schools, but admitted their "obvious constitutional difficulties."

Throughout his campaign Reagan told audiences, which invariably responded with standing ovations, that he would "restore God to public schools." He used the issue of prayer and Bible-reading in the schools effectively in many states, though critics charged him with sheer demagoguery, misrepresentation of the Supreme Court's decisions, and simplistic, shallow theology.

Georgia's former Governor Jimmy Carter, whose sweeping triumphs throughout the crucible of a grueling primary season were nothing short of miraculous, can be credited, however, with reintroducing the "religious issue" into national politics. Overcoming an early reticence to discuss his personal religion, Carter answered the questions of perplexed journalists in great detail. He called himself a "born-again Christian" who underwent "a deep religious experience" which changed his life and gave him "an inner assurance." He admitted to actually liking to attend church, teach Sunday school, and engage in lay missionary activity.

Critics soon pounced on the issue and had a field day throughout the spring and summer. Some sniped that Carter might be dangerous, that he had a "messianic complex" that would cause him to regard his every political decision as the will of God. Arthur Schlesinger, Jr., suggested that "what is really troubling is the implication that evangelical principles can solve social, economic, and international perplexities."[4] Joseph Kraft railed against "Baptist fundamentalism" and suggested that Carter would run poorly "in areas where Baptist rhetoric runs way behind bread and ideology."[5]

Some individuals worried not so much about Carter as about a resurgence of political evangelicalism, of which

Carter is a symbol. The belief that evangelicals in the past were only too wont to use the state to enforce distinctive elements of their moral code on the rest of society caused disquiet among Jews, Catholics, religious liberals, and nonevangelical Protestants. Nonevangelicals remembered that throughout nineteenth-century America, and especially from about 1850 to 1930, evangelical Protestants lobbied for Prohibition, immigration restriction, exclusion of Catholics, Jews, and liberals from public office, Protestant religious exercises in public schools, film and book censorship, and rigid Sunday observances. There was a certain cultural arrogance among these Protestants, who regarded this country as "their country" and religious dissenters as outsiders, whose views should be ignored.

There were those, on the other hand, who believed that Carter was being unfairly harassed by critics who were veering dangerously close to violating Article VI of the U.S. Constitution which prohibits religious tests for public office. Others felt that Carter was so sincere and honest that he was disarming. George F. Will said that "some people suspect that he is guilty of sincerity."[6] *Christianity Today* (April 9, 1976) wondered "whether in a political scene saturated with situationism, a candidate who promises to be honest can survive."

Carter assured audiences that "I've never tried to use my position as a public official to promote my beliefs and I never would."[7] He repeatedly affirmed his belief in strict separation of church and state, a basic Baptist tenet. He opposed public aid to religious schools and government prayer amendments. He endorsed civil disobedience for religious reasons but suggested that conscientious objectors be prepared to take the legal consequences for their actions. He promised strong support for modern Israel, "the fulfillment of Biblical prophecy." He opposed outlawing abortion by constitu-

tional amendment but promised to expand sex education, family planning, and adoption programs to mini-
mize the need for abortion. On balance Carter was the
strongest religious libertarian and church-state separationist since John F. Kennedy.

The most exciting political possibility of the election
year was the "sleeping giant" of American politics, the
evangelical vote. Whether Jimmy Carter could substantially cut into this historically Republican constituency
was "the" political question. There was evidence that he
could. He ran exceptionally well in the evangelical
strongholds of Pennsylvania, Maryland, Iowa, Illinois,
Indiana, and Michigan, in addition to his southern base.
A *Time*-Yankelovich poll conducted nationwide shortly
after the April 27 Pennsylvania primary found that 32%
of the voters considered Carter's religion an asset, while
only 8% felt it to be a liability.[8] Conversely, Carter did
not run well in Oregon, Rhode Island, and New York,
where there are few evangelical voters.

Though Carter's image of decency, honesty, and integrity appealed to evangelical voters, it would not be
known until Election Day whether his political populism-
liberalism could shake their basic political conservatism.
Evangelical political scientist Perry C. Cotham, in his
Politics, Americanism, and Christianity (Baker Book House,
1976), speaks for many evangelicals. "There is no allu-
sion in the New Testament to a government concerned
with social justice, equal rights under law, the distribution of power, wealth or natural resources, or welfare
services." Individuals who believed that would vote Republican.

Most Americans, accustomed to compartmentalize
seemingly incompatible areas of life like religion and
politics, were amazed to see the reintroduction of an old
issue, once thought dead, into the political arena. That
it did reemerge in a secular era is remarkable. Theolo-

gian Charles P. Henderson, Jr., observes: "The subtle intermixing of the sacred and the secular is a constant element in Presidential politics. . . . While all the candidates say that religion is not a factor, there is a subliminal, symbiotic relationship between the two realms."[9]

There is little historical evidence that any of our Presidents have allowed their personal religious sentiments to affect substantially their public-policy decisions. But there is evidence that with the exception of Jefferson, the Adamses, and Wilson, most of them were uninterested in religion and theologically uninformed.

Historian Robert S. Alley has categorized our Presidents into three distinct religious traditions:

Type A includes those in the Congregational-Unitarian tradition, with its emphasis on enlightened humanism; they were "goal-oriented" in approach, "vigorously repudiating the restrictive proclivities" of institutional religion. These are the church-state separationists who gave us the First Amendment, men such as John Adams, Jefferson, Madison, John Quincy Adams, and Lincoln.

Type B are the legalistic Calvinists, who propounded and implemented the messianic concept of government. Those in this tradition felt that "national success was dependent upon a national righteousness." Alley says that this "Calvinism sought to implement a king's chapel in a king's court without the religious establishment." Presidents of this type include Jackson, Grant, Cleveland, McKinley, Theodore Roosevelt, Wilson, Harding, Coolidge, Hoover, Truman, Eisenhower, Johnson, and Nixon.

Type C are the Anglican-Catholic pragmatic idealists, who emphasized realism and situation ethics. These Presidents, such as Washington, Pierce, Arthur, Franklin Roosevelt, and Kennedy, "viewed politics and religion in perfect harmony, each with its own sphere." This approach "takes the institutions of religion seriously, positively." Freed of narrow orthodoxy or utopian ideologizing, "the third way is one that allows for freedom in movement from church to state and back again."[10]

9

Political Profiles
of America's Religious Groups

In this chapter I endeavor to draw brief summary sketches of the political interests and voting patterns of some of America's religious bodies. The profiles are my own creation, based upon wide reading and considerable activity in the general field of religion and politics. The viewpoint is that of a journalist–political scientist, which I am, and not that of an ecclesiologist, which I am not. I have made no attempt to explore the richness and diversity of the religious heritage of our various religious groups. Undoubtedly I have oversimplified the picture and drawn conclusions to which legitimate and significant exceptions can be made. I realize this is so and apologize for it in advance.

Nevertheless, I believe there is a certain validity to what I here attempt. There are doctrinal factors and social and ethical emphases in certain religious traditions that do have political implications. There are also nonreligious sociological factors that tend to characterize certain religious groups which have some bearing on how they are likely to vote on particular issues. In fact, the identification of such factors indicates that in certain Presidential elections they have been highly influential, and doubtless will continue to be.

These profiles do not include all the religious groups that have proliferated in the free religious climate of

America. I have attempted, however, to include all those about which some concrete political facts are known. I regret the omission of Eastern Orthodoxy, which claims over three million adherents in America, but I have found no viable data concerning its political orientation and activity.

CATHOLICS

America's forty-eight-million-strong Roman Catholic community has long favored the Democratic Party. Since the days of Jefferson and Jackson, and especially since Al Smith and Franklin D. Roosevelt, a majority of Catholic voters have regarded the Democrats as the vehicle to achieve their political objectives. There were many reasons for this. Catholics were mostly poor immigrants (eighty percent of the Catholics are still first-, second-, or third-generation Americans)[1] who saw the Whigs and later the Republicans as hostile landlords who barely tolerated them. The Democrats were more inclined to support progressive economic measures and free, open immigration. The linking of anti-Catholic societies to the Republican Party was more than casual and Catholics knew it. Northern Republicans were the "Protestant Party" and no Catholic need apply.

Catholics were more favorably received by local Democratic parties, where they often seized the reins of power. Catholics were appointed to Presidential cabinets by Democrats and even as chief justices of the Supreme Court (Edward Douglass White, Roger Brooke Taney) by Democrats. The disparity continued well into the twentieth century. A study of federal judge appointments under Republicans Harding, Coolidge, and Hoover reveals that only 4% were given to Catholics. Under Roosevelt and Truman, appointments rose to 25%. In some parts of the country no Catholic had ever been named a federal judge before 1933.[2]

Foreign policy issues occasionally created defections among certain Catholic ethnic groups—e.g., among Germans and Irish against Wilson in 1916. In 1920, French and Italian Catholics joined the defection to Republican Harding, but this was a temporary deviation. Al Smith and Franklin D. Roosevelt won a whopping majority among Catholic voters. Smith brought millions of new voters to the Democratic Party. As Samuel Lubell once wrote, "Smith may be today's 'Forgotten Warrior' but the line he drew across the map of American politics has never been erased."[3]

Though most Catholics remained moderate or liberal Democrats, a small but vocal number gravitated toward right-wing, anti-Communist causes. Surveys in the late 1930's showed a higher percentage of Catholics sympathizing with Father Coughlin's political movement than Protestants or Jews. Similarly more Catholics then non-Catholics supported Franco in the Spanish Civil War. Lubell found that 10% to 15% of all Catholics and Jews moved in mutual antipathy, Catholics toward the right and Jews toward the left.[4]

The anti-Communist fervor, stimulated by the Vatican, of many nationality groups propelled a segment of the Catholic community toward the right. Vincent P. de Santis discovered a considerable body of "angry Catholics" who supported Republican Senator Joseph McCarthy in the late 1940's and early 1950's. They were never a majority, however.[5]

Probably about 45% to 50% of Catholics are and have remained liberal Democrats; 30% to 35% are conservative Democrats, particularly in the South and in northern cities. The remaining 20% are conservative Republicans à la William Buckley. Liberal Republicanism has been an upper-class WASP phenomenon, with a considerable Episcopalian and Congregationalist tinge. A few liberal

Republican Catholics, such as Congressmen Conte of Massachusetts and Gude of Maryland, will occasionally appear on the surface, but they are rare.[6]

A conservative Republican trend briefly seemed to captivate American Catholics during the late 1960's. It was so pronounced that Kevin Phillips posited the thesis that Catholics were ripe for picking by Republicans and would constitute an integral part of "the emerging Republican majority." The extravagant claims advanced by Phillips have fallen on barren soil, but they were provocative for a season or two.

It now appears in retrospect that the enormous Catholic swing against McGovern was only a temporary deviation from the norm. Though Nixon swept over 60% in the ethnic wards of many cities, including Philadelphia, New York, Chicago, and Baltimore, these same voters returned to the Democratic banner in 1974.

Andrew M. Greeley believes that Catholics are more liberal than ever, though his view is a minority one. "There has been a dramatic shift to the left in Catholic political and social attitudes over the last two decades," he maintains. Greeley also found strong Democratic loyalties, though "the generation that has come of political age in the last decade is far more likely to be independent than its predecessors."[7]

A Twentieth Century Fund study, on the other hand, concluded that Catholics have "become less liberal and more internally divided" since the Eisenhower era. "Catholics are spread across the attitude continuum," the researchers determined, but a modest swing toward conservatism is perceptible.[8] The same political scientists discovered "no evidence of a shift toward the Republican party among Catholics. If there is a weakening of Democratic identification among some subgroups of Catholics, the movement is into the independent category."[9]

Though Catholics switched to Nixon in 1968 and 1972 in greater numbers than did any other religious group, there is evidence that this may have been a temporary aberration. Lawrence Fuchs believes that a moderate Catholic liberalism is implicit in the Catholic way of life. "For Catholics, religious values have affected presidential choice in the twentieth century through encyclicals supporting the general idea of a welfare state to protect against the misery of old age, unemployment and poverty. Catholic theologians and leaders have always believed that the state has the moral authority to organize economic life, and Franklin Roosevelt, in his first campaign, justified New Deal proposals by appealing to Catholic political theories based on Pope Leo XIII's teachings and given wide circulation in the United States by the late Msgr. John A. Ryan. The liberal economic measures advanced by FDR after his election had been propounded by American Catholic bishops as early as 1917 when they called for a heavier graduated income tax, social security, unemployment insurance and minimum wage legislation."[10]

Though this seems reasonable, there is also some evidence of widespread Catholic discontent over the two primary articles on the Catholic agenda: parochial school aid and abortion. Even such a distinguished liberal as Notre Dame President Theodore Hesburgh gave vent to some rather angry emotions in a 1974 address: "Lately, I have perceived some stirrings among these quiet, faithful, patriotic, modest American Catholics. They are beginning to feel set upon, ignored, even badly used and unappreciated. Let me illustrate from the past year's happenings. Last year, fifty million American Catholics wanted two things, first some help—even modest—to the parochial schools that educated many of their children as they desired, and secondly, no liberalization of the laws on abortion. What happened? The Catholics were denied help to parochial schools and abortion was made legal practically on demand for any reason."[11]

Rabbi Marc Tanenbaum of the American Jewish Committee told an audience at the Bicentennial Conference on Religious Liberty in Philadelphia in April 1976 that non-Catholics should consider some modifications and accommodations in their policy so that Catholics would not feel aggrieved.

Explicit appeals to Catholic voters were made by several leaders in California Governor Jerry Brown's Presidential campaign in Maryland. In predominantly Catholic Prince Georges County, the local Democratic organization endorsed Brown, noting that "Brown's Catholicism wouldn't hurt him" among county voters. A local official told the press, "It feels good to be able to vote for a Catholic again."[12] An election day survey conducted by the *Washington Post* revealed that Maryland Catholics favored Brown 56% to 34% over Jimmy Carter. (The eight heavily Methodist counties went 61% to 39% for Carter.)

Some Catholics seemed uneasy about Jimmy Carter's fervent religiosity. Greeley wrote in June 1976: "The Catholic may understand very well that Carter is not anti-Catholic. Yet deep down he remembers all the anti-Catholic Southern Baptist prejudice of the Al Smith and John Kennedy campaigns. Carter's style touches on painful spots and those slowly receding recollections."

Some Catholics continue to think in a rather parochial way. Paul A. Fisher, formerly a staff assistant to Congressman Delaney of New York, called the Catholic vote "a sleeping giant," "the single largest bloc in the American political spectrum" and one that could have "a controlling influence on shaping America's moral climate." He exaggerated the Catholic percentage of the population in his study, claiming 60 million members, or 31% of the population (whereas 48 million is the "official"

Catholic figure, of whom only 25 million to 30 million are considered practicing). He urged Catholics to vote as a bloc on parochial school aid, abortion, and other moral issues. "There is a clear and identifiable Catholic interest in innumerable political issues. . . . Catholics have a moral duty to be unified and resolute in the political sphere to work for the Catholic interest."[13]

Even in the secular antiauthoritarian '70s, some Catholic clergy have been known to endorse candidates from the pulpit, though such a practice must be exceedingly rare. Several priests endorsed Jimmy Carter for the Democratic nomination on the Sunday preceding the Iowa caucuses in January 1976. Carter swept heavily Catholic Carroll County by a 16-1 margin over Sargent Shriver. Carter was erroneously considered to be the most antiabortion candidate by the parish priests. In 1974, "Maine Governor James B. Longley won an endorsement from the pulpit on at least one occasion during the 1974 election when it became known that he attended Catholic Mass every morning without fail."[14]

Needless to say, America's largest religious body will continue to play a key role in the election process. (See Appendix, Table 8.)

JEWS

America's Jews are a political paradox. They are an affluent, highly educated community, including among their adherents a disproportionate number of scientists, professors, doctors, and lawyers, but politically devoted to liberal causes and the Democratic Party. The other high-status religious groups—Episcopalians, Presbyterians, and United Church of Christ—are (or were) quite solidly Republican. Jews have favored progressive-liberal causes since their arrival on U.S. soil, though most voted Republican for President from Abraham Lincoln in 1860 through Theodore Roosevelt and Taft. A slim plurality and then a slim majority favored Woodrow Wilson in 1912 and 1916. Jews were lukewarmly Republican in the early 1920's but shifted heavily to Al Smith in 1928. Considering the tinge of nativism in the Republican Party, it is somewhat surprising that a majority of Jews would have preferred the G.O.P. One explanation is that the Irish Catholic domination of the Democrats prevented a substantial Jewish following.

Another factor was the Republicans' denunciation of anti-Semitism in Romania and Russia in several party platforms. Presidents Hayes, Arthur, and Benjamin Harrison warned the Romanian and Russian governments that the United States regarded anti-Jewish pogroms with grave disfavor. Theodore Roosevelt was adored by Jews, whose U.S. Rabbinical Conference was first welcomed to the White House by Teddy. His successor, William Howard Taft, promised, though he reneged, that he would renegotiate a discriminatory Russian trade treaty.

Franklin D. Roosevelt's commitment to liberal values and his uncompromising resistance to Hitler solidified Jewish support for the Democrats. Many Jewish intellectuals flocked to join the New Deal brain trust. Many Jews were appointed to federal judgeships by the Democrats and to the U.S. Supreme Court itself, beginning with Wilson's nomination of Louis Brandeis. Jewish support for Roosevelt in 1940 and 1944 neared 95%.

In 1948 many Jews were uncomfortable with Harry Truman, some believing that Progressive Henry Wallace was the genuine inheritor of the Franklin D. Roosevelt mantle. Some preferred the Dewey-Warren ticket, especially in Miami, Pittsburgh, and Cincinnati. Wallace won a quarter of the Jewish votes in New York City, carrying a few precincts in the South Bronx, and a fair vote in parts of Los Angeles, where he also carried some precincts. Still at least 65% to 75% of the Jews favored Truman, whose early recognition of Israel and commitment to civil rights were rewarded.

Illinois' urbane and articulate Governor Adlai Stevenson was an indisputable hero to the Jewish community. A Jewish theological seminary in New York named its institute for the study of ethics in his honor in the 1960's. Three of every four Jewish voters preferred Stevenson over war hero General Dwight Eisenhower, who was regarded as amiable but ineffectual. Jews remained loyal to Stevenson in 1956, many Jewish precincts giving him a *greater* victory than in 1952. Jews especially feared the McCarthy-Jenner-Knowland-Nixon wing of the G.O.P. Jews overwhelmingly supported Kennedy, Johnson, and Humphrey and a 1968 poll found Jews about two and a half times more likely to be liberals than the rest of the country.

A small Jewish trickle to the right was noticeable in the late 1960's among the middle and lower classes, who resented black militancy and opposed quota systems to aid blacks in employment and education, which would have hurt Jews, who emphasized academic excellence and open admissions policies. The blatant anti-Semitism of some in the New Left frightened Jews, as did the rising urban crime rate. In New York City, middle-class Jews opposed the civilian review board for police in 1966 and gave Nixon a higher percentage of their votes than did upper-class Jews, who favored the civilian review board. Poorer Jews also opposed "limousine liberal" John Lindsay in both 1965 and 1969, though the progressive mayor handily won the vote of the well-to-do Jews. In 1971 a majority of poorer Jews favored conservative Democrat Frank Rizzo in the Philadelphia mayoralty race over a liberal Republican. Jewish conservatives like Nathaniel Weyl were exultant and predicted a massive swing to the right among a people that British Prime

Minister Disraeli once suggested were "natural conservatives."

The pro-Israel policy of Richard Nixon and Jewish uncertainty about George McGovern produced a record Jewish Republican vote for Nixon in 1972. Still, he won only a third of the Jewish votes. The post-Watergate elections show a return to the Democrats, suggesting that the 1972 vote was an anti-McGovern fluke. Recent revelations of personal anti-Semitic views of both Nixon and Agnew have not endeared Republicans to the Jewish community.

During the 1976 primaries the hearts of most Jews belonged to Washington Senator Henry Jackson, who swept the Jewish vote in Florida, Massachusetts, New York, and Pennsylvania. Jerry Brown whipped Carter 75%-7% in the Maryland primary, with Jackson and Udall splitting the remaining 18%. Many Jews distrusted Jimmy Carter's devout adherence to evangelical Protestantism and fear that they will not fare well in a Carter administration. Some of their distrust is undoubtedly based on a dislike of the South and a belief that "historically, anti-Semitism had its roots in fundamentalist religion."[15]

Richard Reeves says that Jews believe Baptists to be the most "particularistic and intolerant" of America's religious groups. "Carter's problem is domestic—a religious, cultural and social chasm between Southern Fundamentalists and Northern Jews."[16] However, as Levy and Kramer observe: "Candidates will continue to make special appeals to Jewish voters. No serious Presidential candidate, for instance, can afford to be considered anti-Israel. But when all is said and done, Jewish voters will still ask, 'Which candidate is best for the Jews?' And it is hard to imagine that candidate not being a liberal Democrat."[17]

Having demonstrated the Jewish commitment to liberalism, I immediately pose the question: Why? Why would successful, wealthy people vote against their best economic interests? One answer is suggested by the historical experience of persecution in Christian Europe. For centuries conservative, monarchist, Christian nationalist and fascist regimes ruthlessly persecuted Jews. It wasn't until the French and American Revolutions that Jews were liberated. Liberal and left-of-center parties were the saviors of the Jewish people. It hasn't been that long since the Holocaust, and Jewish memories of that horrible event still shape their political attitudes. Anti-Semitism in the United States, as elsewhere, is associated with conservative and right-wing causes.

Another factor is Jewish rejection of asceticism and otherworldliness and a positive assertion of the innate, creative potentialities of human existence. Jews are noted for their concern for the improvement of the quality of life.

The concept of *tsedakah* (charity) is a deeply rooted Jewish value, as is love of learning and respect for intellectual achievement. A concern for social justice results from this orientation. Liberalism is perceived by Jews to embody charitable concern, pro-intellectualism, and a delight in this world's joys.[18] Given this historical experience, Jews should remain politically liberal and will affect the outcome of elections in New York, California, Massachusetts, New Jersey, Illinois, Ohio, and Maryland, where they are strong. (See Appendix, Table 9.)

BAPTISTS

Political analyst Samuel Lubell has said, "Surprisingly, little attention has been paid to the one ethnic element that is currently having the most explosive political impact in the country—the white Southern Baptists."[19]

The literature on Baptist voting behavior is nonexistent. One must search far and wide for tidbits of information. It seems certain that the fast-growing frontier-oriented Baptists were Jefferson-Jackson Democrats until the slavery issue divided Baptists irrevocably. Southerners were loyal Democrats while northern Baptists joined the evangelical realignment toward the Republicans. Two prominent northern Baptist Republicans were President Warren Harding of Ohio (whom most Baptists would like to forget, owing to his scandalous personal life) and Charles Evans Hughes of New York, twice chief justice of the U.S. Supreme Court and Republican Presidential nominee against Woodrow Wilson in 1916.

The heaviest Baptist counties defected from Al Smith in 1928, going to Hoover 59%–41%, but went solidly for Franklin D. Roosevelt and Harry Truman. Baptists were the heaviest Protestant group for Franklin D. Roosevelt over Thomas Dewey in 1944, 64%–36%. Baptists probably gave half their votes to Adlai Stevenson, but John F. Kennedy slipped a little, due to anti-Catholicism. Johnson ran about the same as Kennedy, though running well ahead in counties where anti-Kennedy voting had been strong but losing ground in the rural Deep South, which Goldwater swept.

One perplexing question is the relatively high degree of Catholic-Baptist conflict. It may stem from an indigenous, native white cultural rivalry with an immigrant-based European culture. The vast differences in polity, liturgy, and doctrine between the churches unquestionably reinforced the hostility, as did the treatment of Baptist missionaries in many Latin Catholic lands, where Catholics bitterly resented the intruders. Baptist antiauthoritarianism and antiforeignism are partial explanations. Whatever the ultimate reasons, Baptists have been somewhat more inclined to resist Catholic influences on public policy than other Protestants and to oppose any linkage or cooperation between the institutions of church and state.

Ironically, though, Baptists and Catholics frequently tend to agree on many social and economic issues where their sectarian interests do not clash. They have both moved in a Republican and conservative direction since the early 1960's, giving Goldwater and Nixon relatively high support compared, say, to Dewey and Willkie. Whether their mutual interests will ever merge is doubtful but open to speculation. Both Baptists and Catholics are distrustful of utopianism and have a practical "tragic sense of life," believing that the sheer cussedness of human behavior tends to make the loftiest of human aspirations go awry.

Baptist wariness of big government and the welfare state, wedded to theological conservatism, produced massive rejections of Humphrey and McGovern. A 1968 survey showed Baptists dividing 46% for Nixon, 32% for Wallace, and only 22% for Humphrey. (The heaviest Baptist counties which I surveyed gave Wallace the edge over Nixon 38%–37%.) McGovern ran poorly among Baptists.

The emergence of fellow Baptist Jimmy Carter produced a wholesale swing back to the Democrats this time around. Prominent Baptist clergy and lobbyists worked hard for Carter in the Texas primary. "Financial and moral support spread throughout the Southern Baptist community like ripples in a pond," said reporter Dave Montgomery. Montgomery believes that Carter's sweeping victory was due largely to Baptists. "Carter's image magnetized powerful support from the legions of Texas Southern Baptists who can exercise formidable political force whenever the need arises."[20]

In the Maryland primary some Baptists pushed the religious issue rather hard. Carter's aunt Emily Dolvin of Roswell, Georgia, campaigning in Marlow Heights, practically begged Baptists to vote for her nephew. "If all you Baptists vote for him, he'll get in there because there are more Baptists than anyone. Get all those Baptists out there on Tuesday and vote," she said.[21] Since Baptists are less than 3% of Maryland's population, her appeals fell mostly on deaf ears.

Many Baptist newspaper editors rallied to Carter's defense when the secular press questioned his intense religious devotion. The *Baptist Courier* accused the "liberal Press" of a double standard in urging voters to disregard Kennedy's religion in 1960 but making an issue of Carter's. R. G. Puckett of the *Maryland Baptist* protested against an "apparent smear campaign against Jimmy Carter . . . because he is a Southern Baptist."

Though most Baptists are no doubt delighted by their newfound prestige and recognition, one thoughtful demurrer was expressed by Forrest M. Mims in the *Baptist New Mexican* (May 29, 1976). After admitting that "it's safe to conclude most Baptists are for Carter," Mims warned against bloc voting and "occasional hints from some of our pulpits" (that might) "evolve into full-fledged endorsements." He also told fellow Baptists that a Carter victory would not produce a utopia. He concluded: "Whether he wins or loses, Carter has done us a valuable service. He's shown us how to speak out boldly on issues which concern Christians. He's taught us how to do what we have forgotten."

We should note the growing strength of the white Southern Baptists primarily in the last half century. (Sixty percent of America's blacks are Baptists, but they vote mainly on civil rights and economic issues.) White Southern Baptists are the dominant religion throughout most of the South. Their traditional rivals, the Methodists, have lost ground everywhere. Methodists led Baptists as recently as a decade ago but today, even after adding almost a million members in the merger with the Evangelical United Brethren, they trail Baptists 12.7 million to 10 million. Baptists have gained 3 million members since 1960 while Methodists have lost 1 million.

Many southern counties that were predominantly Methodist as late as 1952 (National Council of Churches survey) are Baptist today. Baptist growth rate has outpaced all others, except in Florida, where migrations from the North have made that state virtually nonsouthern.

Of the 96 counties where Baptists are a majority of the entire population, all but 6 are more homogeneously Baptist today than in 1926, the year of the last reliable U.S. religious census. Some gains are phenomenal. The Baptist percentage of the total population has risen— 39% in Pontotoc County, Mississippi; 29% in Cherokee County, South Carolina; 27% in Livingston parish, Louisiana; and 40% in Union parish, Louisiana. Some counties legitimate the old joke about more Baptists than people in the South.

Other churches have fallen by the wayside. In one of Mississippi's two traditional Catholic strongholds, Harrison County, Baptists have moved into first place, while Catholics have declined 11%. In Rowan County, North Carolina, Baptists have displaced Lutherans from the top spot. In Nelson County, Kentucky, Catholics have dropped 17%, with Baptists closing in on them. In Mecklenburg County, North Carolina (Charlotte), Baptists, in third place in 1926 with 14% of the population, are now first with 31%. Presbyterians are only up from 23% to 24%, and Methodists from 19% to 22%.

This growth obviously has political implications. Though Baptists are staunch supporters of church-state separation and foes of established religion, a kind of "informal establishment" exists in these counties. Baptist historian Glenn T. Miller explains this concept. "An informal establishment exists when one religious group or a number of related groups have the power to determine religious and moral practices within an area. A Roman Catholic state with aid to parochial schools and strong antiabortion laws and a Baptist county that is dry and has prayers in public schools are both examples of informal establishments."[22]

Baptists, though reluctant to involve the state in moral issues generally, are vigorous critics of drinking and gambling, and their organized lobbies are considered quite effective in such states as Texas and North Carolina. Dave Montgomery says of Texas: "Their collective power at the ballot box has been previously demonstrated with knock-out punches of issues such as local option drinking and horse racing. In the state capital full-time Baptist lobbyists are well heard and well heeded."[23]

Baptists spearheaded the effective opposition to parimutuel gambling in referenda in 1962, 1968, and 1974. All three times the antigambling forces were victorious, the last time by a 3–2 majority. Methodists and Churches of Christ were also prominent in the campaigns. John J. Hurt, editor of the *Baptist Standard,* claimed that antigambling safeguards "are essential to a decent society." He declared, "We will not be satisfied with anything less than a clear prohibition." The pro-horse-racing leaders charged that Baptists were using "bully tactics to impose their moral beliefs on generations of Texans to come." The Baptist General Convention retorted and scored the "cheap attempts of gambling proponents to arouse religious prejudice against Baptists."[24] The Baptist-led Christian Action group in North Carolina has also kept that state virtually dry and free of gambling.

Baptists are solidly conservative, though still Democratic—52% to 21% over the Republicans in a 1971 Gallup survey (25% consider themselves Independents). In 1975 the Democrats led 53%–18%, with 27% Independents. But the wretched showing of Humphrey and McGovern demonstrates that they will not automatically support any Democratic candidate. (See Appendix, Table 10.)

METHODISTS

America's eleven million Methodists are the quintessential centrists of the political, cultural, social, and theological spectrum. They are moderates politically, usually dividing their votes between Democrats and Republicans. They are moderate in income and social status, and theologically middle of the road. Perhaps that is why so many politicians are Methodists. They have always ranked first or second in the number of members in Congress.

Methodists are traditionally social action-oriented, a church of workers rather than thinkers or aesthetes. Louis Cassels says of them: "A denomination of doers, they have furnished the leadership for many civic drives, including those that resulted in regulating child labor and granting suffrage to women."[25]

Methodism began officially by separating from the Anglican Church in 1784 and grew rapidly on the frontier where its "circuit riders" (itinerant preachers) were a common feature of the landscape. It was soon the largest Protestant church, and by 1850 two thirds of U.S. Protestants were either Methodists or Baptists. Methodists leaned somewhat to the conservative Federalists and Whigs in the early nineteenth century and, then, like their Baptist counterparts, divided over the Civil War—northern Methodists becoming Republicans; southerners, Democrats. Methodists were the leaders of the evangelical wing of Protestantism for generations and were the foremost advocates of Prohibition and Bible-reading in public schools. Hence, the leading Methodist counties went heavily for Hoover over Smith in 1928.

Sometime in the 1930's Methodism began to veer left and that movement has continued to the present. The Glock-Stark surveys of American religion show Methodists to be consistently liberal in doctrine, and the church's social pronouncements are indisputably liberal.[26] One of its leaders, Bishop James Armstrong, campaigned enthusiastically for McGovern in 1972.

Not all Methodists are happy about the change in the church's direction. A survey conducted by *Interpreter*, a United Methodist journal, found that church members are more conservative theologically and sociologically than the clergy and professional staffs. The 13,000 replies made it clear to church leaders that many Methodists "are bitterly frustrated" about their church's policies and programs.[27]

Methodists are politically right down the center. In 1944 a survey showed Dewey edging Roosevelt 50.4%–49.6%. A 1971 Gallup survey showed 36% of all Methodists to be Democrats, 35% Republicans, and 26% Independents. In 1975 Democrats led 38%–30%, with 30% Independents. In 1968 Gallup showed Methodists voted 57% for Nixon, 29% for Humphrey, and 14% for Wallace—a somewhat heavier Republican vote than anticipated.

There is not the homogeneity in Methodist country that there is in Catholic, Baptist, and Lutheran parts of the nation. There is no county where Methodists are a majority of the population, but there are many counties where they are 30% to 45% of the total. They are strongest in 8 counties on Maryland's Eastern Shore, in rural Delaware, Nebraska, Kansas, parts of Virginia, and West Virginia, the only state where they are the largest religious group. In 36 relatively strong Methodist counties, Eisenhower won 59.6% in 1956 and Nixon 53.2% in 1960. Kennedy's solid 6% gain (he carried 8 of the Eisenhower counties) shows the decline of anti-Catholicism, since these counties gave Al Smith less than 38%. Johnson won a comfortable 58% over Goldwater in 1964 and Nixon beat Humphrey 47.4%–33.8%, with Wallace garnering a rather strong 18.8% in 1968. Nixon whipped McGovern about 70%–30% in 1972.

Many of the above counties had Methodist majorities in 1926. In the 8 Maryland Eastern Shore counties Methodists have dropped from 71% to 58% among church members and are no more than 30% of the total population. In only 5 of the 36 counties are they stronger today than in 1926. In some of the counties they are down 15% to 25%. In many other sections of the South, dozens of Methodist counties have become Baptist strongholds. Even in rural Delaware they are down 21% in Sussex County and 28% in Kent County.

Methodists are still influential and have contributed several Presidents (Hayes, Grant, McKinley) and several Supreme Court justices to the country. Their social activism makes them a political force to be reckoned with where their concerns become issues in any campaign.

LUTHERANS

America's nine million Lutherans are solidly old immigrant stock, being heirs to the emigrations from Germany, Norway, Sweden, Denmark, and Finland. Lutherans are disproportionately concentrated in the Midwest and in Pennsylvania.

The sketchy data we have suggest that Lutheran voting behavior is somewhat more fluid than among other Protestants. A majority probably voted Republican until Franklin D. Roosevelt's New Deal, but progressive and populist liberal Republicanism was more the vogue than the conservative variety. Lutherans resisted the excesses of the abolitionist and prohibitionist movements, since Lutheranism has never been social action conscious or puritanical on drinking. In some elections it seems that German Lutherans responded to foreign policy considerations in one way, the Scandinavians in another. Bob

La Follette edged out President Coolidge in the heaviest Lutheran counties in 1924, but Al Smith did not run well among them. Smith did well among beer-loving Germans, who deeply resented Prohibition, but very poorly among the Scandinavians. Support for economic progressivism gave Roosevelt comfortable majorities in 1932 and 1936, but strong antiwar feelings gave Willkie a landslide in the German counties in 1940. In Norwegian counties Franklin D. Roosevelt still won heavily, due to the resentment of the Nazi invasion of Norway, but in Swedish counties, Willkie won easily. Sweden remained neutral during the war.

In 1944 Dewey edged Roosevelt by about 55%–45%. Harry Truman won in Lutheran areas in 1948, due probably to the farm vote and sectional loyalties.

Eisenhower won comfortably in 1952 and 1956, though Stevenson gained impressively in 1956. Kennedy ran into some traditional Lutheran distrust of Catholicism and ran behind Stevenson in some Swedish and Norwegian counties. Over all, though, he ran 1% better than Stevenson. Barry Goldwater had no appeal here, and in 1968 Humphrey ran stronger among Lutherans than among other Protestant groups. Gallup gave Nixon a 55%–43% edge and the heavy Lutheran counties went for him 55%–45%. Lutherans are somewhat liberal on economic questions and this may account for the relatively good Humphrey showing. McGovern's 41% was also better than his national showing.

Among Lutherans there appears to be a tendency toward noninvolvement in the political arena, shown by the tiny Lutheran contingent in Congress and the absence of Lutherans from the White House.

William Adams Brown, a brilliant theologian of yesteryear, writes of Lutheranism: "Even more consistently than the Anglicans the Lutherans have been ready to accord the state exclusive responsibility in the sphere of social and political action. With few exceptions they have confined the function of the church to witness in the sphere of personal religion and so long as the church was assured of complete freedom in this field it has been willing to give the state its loyal support in the field of politics and economics."[28]

There is survey evidence that a direct correlation exists among Lutherans between theological and political orientation. Lawrence K. Kersten's excellent book *The Lutheran Ethic* shows the connection: "Our data show that clergymen who are theologically more conservative more often 1) identify with the Republican Party; 2) prefer Republican candidates; 3) take a conservative stand against government social welfare; 4) oppose foreign aid; and 5) take a more 'hawkish' stand on war. For Lutheran laymen the higher an individual ranks on the five dimensions of religious commitment, the more likely he is to identify with the Republican Party and prefer Republican candidates. These findings suggest that at least part of the Lutheran ethic continues to exist among the theologically conservative and the religiously most committed Lutherans. Furthermore, the data suggest a strong relationship between a theologically conservative stance and political and social conservatism."[29]

The Kersten survey also reveals Lutherans to be 53%–40% Republican (with 7% Independent). The 1971 Gallup survey gives a similar Republican edge 40%–31%, but shows 29% Independents. Lutheran clergy, however, favor the G.O.P. by about 70%–29%. The more conservative the synod, the higher the G.O.P. identification. Upper-class and well-educated Lutherans are more likely to be liberal in religion and politics. Parochial school graduates are far more likely to be conservative politically and religiously than public school graduates. Lutheran lay people favored Johnson 69%–31% over Goldwater, and the clergy wanted Johnson 64%–36%.

Kersten believes that Lutheranism tends to produce a conservative political outlook. "Political and social conservatism are inherent in the Lutheran ethic. The ethic's view of life regards man as sinful by nature and regards institutions such as government as keeping man's basic corruption and selfishness in check and thereby maintaining order. The government, the varying social classes, the unequal distribution of wealth, and even war are viewed as part of God's divinely willed plan. The ethic views secular reform movements with suspicion because of man's inherent evilness. The religious person is one who humbly submits to the existing social order, attempts to perpetuate the status quo, and welcomes earthly death, which is his only true hope for relief from the bondage of sin."[30]

He also says that "although Lutherans feel strongly about particular moral issues in American society, they rarely act in an organized way to change the conditions that disturb them."[31]

His conclusions seem reasonable to me, but he overstates Lutheran conservatism in the U.S. political context since Lutherans are economically moderate to liberal and have given the last five Democratic Presidential candidates a respectable vote. In 1975, 38% of the Lutherans called themselves Independents, 30% Democrats, and only 29% Republicans—a major Republican decline. (See Appendix, Table 11.)

PRESBYTERIANS

America's four million Presbyterians are found primarily in the middle and upper middle class. They, like the Methodists, are scattered throughout the country and cannot be said to be regional, though Pennsylvania is their historic stronghold, where over half a million reside. The Pittsburgh area (Allegheny County) has the largest concentration (128,000) of Presbyterians in the country. Patches of Presbyterian strength are found elsewhere, notably in Virginia and North Carolina (especially Charlotte). Presbyterians have always emphasized education and social concern. Though Presbyterians make up about 5% of the general adult population, they make up 11% of the college educated, 17% of university faculties, and 19% of the faculty at prestigious colleges.[32] They have had the second highest number of Presidents, including Cleveland, Wilson, Jackson, and Eisenhower, and as Louis Cassels notes: "Presbyterians have taken an active part in civic affairs ever since colonial times. In any legislative body, from a city council to the U.S. Congress, you will find a disproportionate number of Presbyterians."[33]

Presbyterians were strong in colonial America, coming to the United States to flee English and Anglican persecution in Scotland and Ireland. They flocked primarily to Pennsylvania and gave the western and central parts of that state a Scotch-Irish flavor. They almost unanimously supported the War of Independence, so much so that one British general is said to have called the War "a Presbyterian rebellion." Presbyterians were staunch Jefferson-Jackson Democrats until the post Civil War era, when the northerners, who comprised three fourths of all Presbyterians, became Republicans. They have generally remained Republicans since and are relatively conservative on most political issues. High Presbyterian social status has reinforced this Republican loyalty. A study of business executives showed 17% to be Presbyterians.[34] A 1966 family income study showed Presbyterians third behind Jews and Episcopalians.[35]

Presbyterians voted 60%–40% for Dewey over Roosevelt in 1944 and 3 to 1 for Nixon over Humphrey in 1968. A 1971 Gallup survey shows Presbyterians favoring the G.O.P. 45%–28% over the Democrats and 25%

Independent. In 1975 the Republicans dropped to 39%, while Democrats and Independents won 30%. In all surveys they are the most Republican of the major churches. They will likely remain so, even though with other mainline denominations they have suffered membership loss since 1965.

EPISCOPALIANS

America's most elite and prestigious religious community are the Episcopalians, the three million members of the U.S. branch of the Anglican Communion. The once established church in the southern colonies (and New York City for a while) has remained the semi-established church to this day. Ranking first or second on almost all surveys of education and affluence, this group has given the United States more Presidents (11) than anyone else, 6 of the 15 chief justices of the Supreme Court, 34 of the 56 signers of the Declaration of Independence, and about two thirds of the framers of the Constitution. They comprise about 30% of the top business executives[36] and 9% of the faculty at prestigious colleges.[37] Fifty-one of the 91 Supreme Court justices appointed from 1789 to 1957 have been Episcopalians or Presbyterians.[38] As Louis Cassels writes, "If the Episcopal Church still has a special appeal for any one group of Americans, it is for the academic-intellectual-professional community. Large numbers of scientists, doctors, lawyers, writers, college professors, and the like, are to be found in the pews of Episcopal churches."[39]

Episcopalians are urban-suburban and still concentrated heavily on the Eastern Seaboard from Florida to Maine, though they are found all over the United States and in some of the unlikeliest rural areas of the West.[40] Many prominent Virginians, from the earliest Presidents on down to the present, are numbered in the Anglican ranks. Episcopalians are probably still predominantly Anglo-Saxon, though this is diminishing due to the fact that a higher percentage of Episcopalians are converts from other churches, than in any other major denomination. (Forty-one percent of the Episcopalians, compared to 34% of the Presbyterians, 25% of the Lutherans, 20% of the Methodists, 15% of the Baptists, and 9% of the Catholics, are converts from other churches.)[41]

Most Anglican clergy and northern laity were Loyalists during the Revolution, and fled to England or Canada after the war, though southern laymen were leaders in the fight for independence. The church was gravely weakened after 1789 and experienced its greatest growth after World War I. Most Anglicans were probably Federalists and later Republicans, though Connecticut Anglicans voted en bloc in 1811 for the Democrats to protest the cutoff of state funds for their bishop (an early example of self-interest bloc voting).

Episcopalians generally opposed Prohibition, having, as Lipset says, "come out of a tradition of having been a state and total-society church. They never saw their religious mission as prescribing behavior, in the way that the sects or denominations with sectarian origin typically do."[42] Their growth was considerable after 1916, doubling their membership between the two world wars. They almost doubled again between 1950 and 1960, but have lost a half million members since 1965.

Episcopalians lean toward the Republicans and toward economic conservatism but are quite liberal on sociocultural issues, ranking a close third in liberalism on the Glock-Stark scales. They favored Dewey over Roosevelt in 1944 by only 55%–45% and Nixon over Humphrey 54%–39% in 1968. Their party affiliation in 1971 was 44% Republican, 32% Democrat, and 23% Independent. Their relative liberalism is keeping the Republican vote well below reasonable expectations for a high-status group. Episcopalians are far less likely to vote G.O.P. than their social-status rivals, the Presbyterians.

Another reason for this may be that their well-educated clergy "are very liberal in their political views" according to internal church survey data. Many Anglicans in Congress are liberals, but many Anglican politicians, including Barry Goldwater, Gerald Ford, and Spiro Agnew, have been ideological conservatives. In 1975, 34% of the Episcopalians called themselves Independents, 33% Republicans, and 30% Democrats—a significant Republican decline.

THE UNITED CHURCH OF CHRIST

This amalgam of New England Congregationalists and Swiss-German Evangelicals still has considerable prestige, though its membership has fallen below two million. Its one President, Calvin Coolidge, embodied the conservative, Calvinistic orientation of American Congregationalists. These moralistic New Englanders were devoted abolitionists and prohibitionists and quite distrustful of Catholicism. In 1944 they voted 70%–30% for Thomas Dewey over Franklin D. Roosevelt, the most Republican showing of the major churches. They have not been included in recent surveys, so one can only surmise their present political leanings.

This group in one generation or so has moved from *status quo* conservatism to fierce theological and social liberalism. Its members are the most liberal in the Glock-Stark surveys and its church agencies are consistently liberal (even approving the ordination of avowed homosexuals to the ministry). This would surely affect voting behavior and it is significant that Democrats have almost tripled their percentage of United Church of Christ members in Congress since 1961.

There are no adequate data on this group alone, but

a clue is found in Kevin Phillips' description of certain "Yankee Protestant" counties in 15 states, where Congregationalists and other northern Protestants settled and fashioned a distinctive cultural milieu. These counties are found in Oregon, South Dakota, Iowa, Wisconsin, Kansas, and Missouri as well as New England. They have been rock-ribbed Republican for a century or more, usually by 2 to 1 margins. Al Smith's 24% was the low-water mark. In 1932 they still adored Hoover 60.5%–39.5% over Roosevelt. In fact, neither Franklin D. Roosevelt nor Wilson ever achieved 40%. Truman and Kennedy won only a third and Stevenson a fourth of their vote. (Anti-Catholicism must have diminished since John F. Kennedy ran 9% ahead of Stevenson.) In 1964, these counties deserted Barry Goldwater in droves, voting 56.4% for Johnson, the first Democratic winner ever. The increasing liberalism began to be reflected in Presidential voting. Humphrey won 38.4%, better than Franklin D. Roosevelt's last two tries. McGovern ran exceptionally well in 1972 (36.7%). The liberal Democratic trend is likely to continue in this constituency, where theological liberalism has shaped a new generation of voters.

THE REFORMED CHURCHES

About 600,000 Americans of Dutch and German descent are members of two Reformed churches—the very conservative Christian Reformed Church, centered in Michigan and Iowa, and the moderate Reformed Church in America, which has many members in the Old Dutch Hudson River Valley of New York and upper New Jersey. Politically they are quite conservative and Republican. Norman Vincent Peale, the popular preacher, and the late Republican Senator Everett Dirksen of Illinois are examples of the Reformed tradition. These churchgoers accept the underlying presuppositions of evangelical cultural values and add a Calvinist reinforcement.

One explanation for Calvinist conservatism, which may affect Presbyterians and Reformed Church members who take their religion seriously, is a tendency to identify prosperity with godliness. Calvinistic thinking on social matters has tended toward a belief that material prosperity is a presumptive sign of God's favor, while poverty is a sign of divine disapproval. Such an attitude presupposes that social welfare is really unnecessary and perhaps irreligious. Furthermore, a distrust of revolution and change can be inferred from a Calvinist world view. One of Calvinism's most trenchant thinkers, Dr. Abraham Kuyper, premier of Holland in the early days of the twentieth century, actually called his political movement the Anti-Revolutionary Party. An acceptance of unchanging morality and ethics wedded to an ethic of sobriety, industry, and thrift in personal relationships may contribute to attitudes of political conservatism. Reformed Church members are also relatively well-to-do, ranking in the 1945 Princeton study above Methodists, Lutherans, Baptists, and Mormons and only a little behind Episcopalians, Presbyterians, and Congregationalists.

Calvinism's church-state orientation is ironically closer to Roman Catholicism than to Eastern Orthodoxy, Anglicanism, or Lutheranism. William Adams Brown observes: "To Calvin . . . the church was in a true sense God's representative on earth and its authority extended to all phases of man's life. It was the church's function . . . to see that God's will was obeyed, not only in the life of the individual, but so far as is possible in society."[43]

Three counties, Sioux in Iowa, and Ottawa and Missaukee in Michigan, are overwhelmingly Reformed and can be used for our analysis. (There are also substantial Reformed populations in Kent County [Grand Rapids],

Michigan; Marion County, Iowa; Whatcom County, Washington; and Douglas County, South Dakota.) With the exceptions of FDR's win in 1932 and 1936, these Dutch Reformers are fervently Republican. Eisenhower swept 76%, and Nixon a slightly larger 77%. (A Dutch *Catholic* town, Little Chute in Outagamie County, Wisconsin, gave Kennedy 73%, compared to Stevenson's 31%.) Even Goldwater won a comfortable 57%. Nixon won 75% over Humphrey and McGovern, though McGovern ran an eyelash ahead of Humphrey.

MORMONS

One of America's fastest growing religious groups is the Utah-based Church of Jesus Christ of Latter-day Saints, who now claim 2.7 million adherents, a figure more than double their 1960 strength. This indigenous, family-oriented, and fiercely patriotic group dominates every county in Utah, all but 5 in Idaho, 3 in Wyoming (Big Horn, Lincoln, and Uinta), 2 in Nevada (Lincoln, White Pine), and 2 in Arizona (Graham, Navajo). They have fluctuated historically, generally going for the winner, but have become rather solidly Republican since Eisenhower. Kennedy did well, receiving 45% or so in 1960, as Al Smith had done in 1928. Many Mormons may have felt a kinship for another minority whose loyalty was being questioned. Johnson edged Goldwater, but only gained 4% in the Idaho counties. Goldwater was relatively popular among Mormons. Nixon crushed Humphrey and McGovern, and Republican candidates should continue to do well among this congenial congerie of conservatives.

CHRISTIAN SCIENTISTS

Little is known about the political preferences of this 300,000-member, indigenous religious group, among whose adherents is numbered Senator Charles Percy of Illinois. Their high social status (near the top in the 1945-46 Princeton survey) and adherence to traditional Protestant sociocultural mores would likely produce strong Republican voting. Their fear of Catholicism could not have helped Kennedy in 1960. My 1974 survey, which included a large number of Christian Scientists, found an overwhelming Republican identification and a 92% vote for Nixon in both 1968 and 1972.

SEVENTH-DAY ADVENTISTS

The half million or so members of this American-based religious group are concentrated on the Pacific Coast, one third of their members living in California, Oregon, or Washington. They have some political clout in Walla Walla County, Washington, and Umatilla County, Oregon.

Little is known about their political views, but several church officials expressed a belief that Adventists are mostly conservative Republicans. They adhere to the cultural values of evangelical Protestantism and frown on moral permissiveness, omnicompetent government, secular public education, and any linkage or cooperation between church and state. They believe fervently in absolute religious liberty and feel that this freedom can only be maintained through a total separation of church and state. They are strongly antiecumenical.

Another reinforcement toward Republicanism is Adventist disdain for labor unions, which generally influence the Democratic Party. Adventists believe in right-to-work laws and oppose compulsory unionism. Republican candidates are the most likely to agree with that position. This policy toward trade unions is theologically based, since Adventists believe that employee-employer relationships should be based on love and trust. Elder Melvin Adams expresses it this way: "The Scriptural statement that the servant of the Lord must not be 'unequally yoked' (II Cor. 6:14) is very meaningful to these people. Consequently, they are opposed to being bound together with non-Christians in organizations that require them to support certain policies and courses of action that violate their religious convictions."[44]

My 1974 survey indicated top-heavy Republican majorities and pro-Nixon voting. Nixon topped 82% in 1968, with Wallace edging out Humphrey for second place. He beat McGovern 9-1 in 1972, though more Adventists abstained from voting than any other religious group. They were apparently disillusioned by Nixon's pro-Catholic policies on parochiaid and abortion but couldn't bring themselves to vote for McGovern. They will probably continue to favor the G.O.P.

UNITARIANS

Though there are only 175,000 Unitarian Universalists in the United States, their influence has been surprisingly strong. Perhaps the best-educated and most theologically and politically liberal church, Unitarians are well represented in Congress, the Hall of Fame, and the Presidency. The New England base of Unitariansim produced a Republican orientation, though a liberal one, Elliot Richardson style. No data are available but it would seem that Unitarians have been voting Democratic since Franklin D. Roosevelt. Unitarian solons (with the glaring exception of Nebraska Republican Senator Roman Hruska) are consistently liberal. The humanistic, nondogmatic, civil libertarian orientation of Unitarian thought ratifies and reinforces, if it does not produce, political liberalism. A survey of Unitarians discovered that 57% "generally support the Democratic Party" and that 74% voted for Johnson over Goldwater.[45]

A WORD ABOUT "THE EVANGELICALS"

The term "evangelical" has many meanings. It connotes the basic orientation of all Christians to share the gospel with others, but it has come to be identified with the conservative wing of Protestantism, which emphasizes the authority and inerrancy of the Bible. Evangelicals, who enjoyed a period of cultural and political dominance in the United States from about 1850 to 1930, also came to be identified with moral righteousness, social reform aimed at moral regeneration, and preservation of the *status quo* once a reasonably moral society had been created.

Evangelicalism, which always crossed denominational lines, declined until the mid- and late-1960's, when it regained its lost respectability. It is universally conceded to be the fastest growing religious movement in America today and may number 40 million to 50 million adherents under its umbrella. Dean Kelley, a Methodist official with the National Council of Churches, believes that Evangelicalism's rebirth can be explained by its unwillingness to compromise away essentials, its stress on demanding a high level of commitment from believers, and a desire to win others to the cause.[46]

For example, in the last ten years, liberal or moderate bodies (American Baptist, American Lutheran, Disciples of Christ, Episcopal, Lutheran Church in America, Presbyterians, Methodists, United Church of Christ) have lost ground considerably while such conservative bodies as Assemblies of God, independent Baptists, Southern

Baptists, Missouri and Wisconsin Synod Lutherans, Churches of God, Salvation Army, and Nazarenes have boomed. Since 1965 liberal and moderate religious bodies have lost 9% in membership while conservative groups have grown more than 20%. These percentages may even understate the true picture, because there are evangelicals in most of the moderate-liberal denominations but very few liberals in the conservative ones.[47]

The political implications of the evangelical resurgence are potentially significant. If 20% of the voters are evangelicals, this means that 16 million of the 80 million votes expected to be cast in national elections will be evangelical votes, a bloc of considerable impact.

Evangelical voters are strongly concentrated in 11 southern states and 6 border ones (Maryland, West Virginia, Delaware, Kentucky, Missouri, and Oklahoma). They are also found in fairly large numbers in several Midwestern and North-Central states (such as Illinois, Indiana, Iowa, Kansas, and Nebraska). The southern and border states have 177 electoral votes, and Indiana, Iowa, Kansas, and Nebraska have 33, for a total of 210. This is short of the 270 needed for election, but evangelicals in other states (Ohio and Pennsylvania, for example) could provide the victory margin in a close election.

My research, based on a county and precinct study of election returns, correlated with church membership and voting on sensitive religious-oriented referendum questions, suggests that evangelicals have favored the Republican Presidential nominees for at least a generation or more.

It seems likely that Hubert Humphrey and George McGovern received only 15% to 20% of the evangelical vote in the last two elections. If so, it means that about 3 million evangelicals voted for McGovern in 1972 compared to 13 million for Nixon.

Fundamentalists are often included in the evangelical category, though their separatism, anti-intellectualism, and tendencies toward extremism in religion push them generally toward far-right candidates. Fundamentalist support for extreme right political movements is revealed by the resolutions adopted by the World Congress of Fundamentalists in Edinburgh in June 1976. The mostly American and British delegates denounced all other religious movements, the news media, women's liberation, modern translations of the Scriptures, modern church music, situation ethics, socialism, detente, the ecumenical movement, and the World Council of Churches. They endorsed capital punishment and strict Sunday observances. They "supported the stand taken by the Fundamentalists in Northern Ireland . . . as they refuse to surrender their Protestant heritage and their majority right." The delegates "repudiated" the "blasphemies, idolatries and superstitions of Roman Catholicism which anger God and damn the soul."[48] It is obvious that Catholic candidates would not do well among these voters. (See Appendix, Table 12.)

THE RELIGIOUSLY NONAFFILIATED

Technically, the 38% of Americans who decline to affiliate with an organized religious body are the largest segment of the electorate. Unfortunately, this category includes all kinds of people: atheists, agnostics, humanists, free thinkers, and those who reject institutional religion; the present-day Laodiceans who never give ultimate values a thought; those who are searching for meaningful religious experiences; individualists who prefer their own noninstitutional religion; and millions who consider themselves churchgoers even if they only appear at Christmas and Easter and do not officially identify with a local congregation.

Church membership data reported by the *Yearbook of American and Canadian Churches, 1976* show 62% of all Americans to be church members, but 71% claim to be members in the 1976 Gallup survey. Similar results were obtained in the 1957 sample survey of religion conducted by the U.S. Census Bureau.

The Gallup Opinion Index reveals that individuals with no religious preference are mostly males, under age thirty, of moderate income and relatively well educated —42% are college graduates, a figure about comparable to the Presbyterians. Politically, the nonaffiliated are more likely to be Independents (49%) than Democrats (36%) or Republicans (9%).

There is some indication that the nonaffiliated are more politically liberal than most churchgoers, especially among the young and college educated. Several Yankelovich surveys of young people show a positive correlation between rejection of formal religion and political liberalism.[49] On sociocultural values more than economic questions there is a tendency toward liberalism or radicalism and rejection of tradition. Gallup and Harris polls substantiate this.

Another significant survey was conducted by Philip P. Ardery on twelve representative American campuses from 1961 to 1963 and replicated during the 1969-70 academic year. It shows a strong connection between religious and political liberalism. The lengthy survey, based on one designed in 1959 for the *Harvard Crimson* by sociologist David Reisman, found students who rejected traditional Christianity and Judaism were fervently liberal on abortion, sex, international affairs, civil rights and liberties, socialization of basic industries, recognition of Communist China, and national health insurance. Indeed, they were much more liberal than religiously practicing students.[50]

My 1974 survey of 1,700 members of a large national

organization revealed a rather startling difference between the religiously nonaffiliated and conventional religious types. Traditional religionists (almost all Protestants in this survey) gave Nixon 86% against Humphrey and 87% against McGovern. (Less than 8% had favored Wallace, so I am giving only the major-party vote.) Those with no affiliation favored Nixon 60%–40% over Humphrey but only 57%–43% over McGovern. McGovern was favored by 82% of Jews, 72% of humanists-atheists, 65% of Unitarians, 43% of the nonaffiliated, but less than 13% of the religiously conservative or moderate. Among Protestants, McGovern ranged from a high 22% of Methodists, down to less than 10% of Baptists, Christian Scientists, and fundamentalists.

A college education is generally conceded to be a liberalizing experience, especially for those who attend the prestigious universities. Survey data from many sources confirm a predominance of liberal sentiment on virtually all social and political issues. On the other hand, college-educated people are generally affluent and tend to vote Republican to a much greater extent than others. This pro-Republican factor vanished in the 1972 election, as George McGovern ran as well among the college educated as with the general electorate—the first time a Democrat had done so. His greatest triumphs often came in university precincts throughout the nation.

In my survey McGovern ran 1% better than Humphrey among the college educated. He ran 18% better among the college educated than among the grammar school educated. (George Wallace, not unexpectedly, did three times better among the grammar school educated than among college graduates.) Religiously, McGovern swept 79% of college-educated Jews, Unitarians, and humanists (Humphrey won 77%) and 53% of the college-educated nonaffiliated (compared to only 44% for Humphrey). Interestingly, a large pro-McGovern anti-trend surfaced among the college-educated Methodists, who gave McGovern 5% more than Humphrey.

We can safely say that the available evidence, however sketchy, strongly suggests that the religious left prefers the political left. It is undoubtedly related to a this-worldly concern for political and social justice and a passion for experimentation. Continued support for liberal-socialist political measures among this influential segment of the electorate can probably be expected.

A CONCLUDING OBSERVATION

The Gallup Opinion Index's latest survey on religion is sobering reading for Republicans. The post-Watergate decline of Republican identification, especially among Protestants, is pronounced. In just four years, from 1971 to 1975, Republican support among Episcopalians and Lutherans has fallen 11%. Among Presbyterians the Republican decline is 6%, while among Methodists it is 5% and Baptists 3%. Among Catholics, Republicans are 5% weaker, but among Jews they are 2% stronger. (Still, less than one Jew in 12 identifies with the G.O.P.)

The Democrats haven't done too well, either. They have generally held their own among Protestant groups. Among Catholics and Jews, Democrats are somewhat weaker than in 1960. It is the Independents who have gained significantly, and no one knows what this portends for the future of party politics in America. (See Appendix, Table 13.)

10

Representation and Influence
in Congress

Most of this book deals with the ways in which religion may influence one's choice of political candidates. There are two other areas in which religion may be influential: in the formation of public policy decisions by the Congress and in political issues decided by referendum. We shall begin with an overview of the religious configuration of the present Congress. We shall then look first at a few issues in Congress that have had religious significance.

RELIGIOUS AFFILIATION
OF THE MEMBERS OF CONGRESS

Prior to 1960 there was little systematic interest in maintaining records of the denominational affiliations of the members of Congress. Minority groups, such as Jews and Roman Catholics, tended to maintain their own records, partially to indicate increasing acceptance for their coreligionists in a heavily Protestant country. Stephen D. Isaac's *Jews and American Politics*, for example, records all the Jewish members since the 1st Congress.

After the 1960 election *Christianity Today*, the Washington, D.C.-based evangelical fortnightly, began an annual survey of the religious affiliation of members of Congress. Religious News Service has cooperated in gathering these vital data. Fragmentary data prior to 1960 indicated that Methodists tended to have the largest Congressional representation, with Roman Catholics slowly gaining strength.

The 1960 data revealed that Roman Catholics had moved into first place, with a 99–95 edge over Methodists. This trend has intensified throughout the last decade and a half. The Congress elected in 1974 shows Roman Catholics well ahead of second-place Methodists 124–85. There was no correlation between Roman Catholic membership in Congress and the Democratic landslide of 1964 and the Republican landslide of 1972. Catholics picked up members after each election, while Methodists and Presbyterians declined after both. The year 1972 may have been a fluke, however, since the 1974 Democratic sweep showed Roman Catholics, Jews, and Unitarians gaining substantially, while Presbyterians declined significantly. Similar results occurred after the 1964 Democratic win. (See Appendix, Table 14.)

One factor that interests religious sociologists is the relative overrepresentation or underrepresentation of the major religious groups. For example, the data for the 94th Congress reveal that high-status Unitarians, Episcopalians, Presbyterians, and United Church of Christ members were heavily overrepresented, while Lutherans were the most underrepresented major group. Jewish representation has fluctuated, from 11 in the 88th Congress to 24 in the 94th. Generally it is a bit higher than their share of the total population. Roman Catholic representation is right on target, about 22% to 23% of both Congress and the nation.

The underrepresentation of Lutherans raises some serious questions. There has never been a Lutheran President, nor even a Lutheran Presidential candidate of a major party. There have been very few Lutheran cabinet members and Lutheran justices of the Supreme Court.

Two of the major Democratic contenders for President in 1976, Senator Henry Jackson of Washington and Senator Lloyd Bentsen of Texas are descendants of Norwegian and Danish Lutheran families, respectively. And yet both are Presbyterians. And Walter Mondale's forebears were Norwegian Lutherans, but became Methodists. One of the unanswered questions of religion and politics in America is why underrepresentation of Lutherans in Congress and why has it been falling steadily?

Another grossly underrepresented group are those 38% of Americans who are without a formal religious affiliation. Only 6 members of Congress, or slightly over 1%, claim no affiliation, and this is the high figure since 1960. It may be that there is subtle social pressure requiring some sort of religious identification which politicians feel is desirable. I suspect that the 17 "Protestant" members of Congress are really without any significant religious commitment. When there are over 250 varieties of Protestantism in this country, it seems singularly imprecise to designate oneself merely as Protestant. (See Appendix, Table 15.)

The party breakdown by religion in Congress is most instructive, as it tends to reflect what we have already tentatively concluded from previous election results. Baptists, Jews, Roman Catholics, and Unitarians are heavily Democratic. Methodists have a Democratic edge while Episcopalians and Presbyterians have a Republican edge, except in Democratic landslide years. Lutheran and United Church of Christ delegations lean toward the Republican side, though less so than in previous years. The only anomaly here is that Lutheran voters give the Democrats a respectably large share of their Presidential vote, which does not seem to be reflected in the Congressional data.

The 1972 elections revealed a slowly increasing pro-Republican trend among Baptists and Roman Catholics, a majority of whom had just voted for Richard Nixon. Twenty-nine percent of Roman Catholic members of Congress were Republicans during the 93rd Congress, a figure double the percentage of Catholic Republicans in 1960. Especially in Illinois, New York, and New Jersey were many first-term Catholic Congressmen elected. The 1974 election showed a return to normalcy as only 20% of the Catholic representatives were members of the G.O.P. Eighteen more Catholic Democrats were elected, and 8 fewer Catholic Republicans. Among Baptists, 29% were Republicans after the Nixon sweep, but only 23% were after the 1974 returns were counted.

There is a long-range Democratic trend among the United Church of Christ, Unitarian, "Protestant," Lutheran, and Presbyterian groups. A smaller Republican trend among Baptists and Roman Catholics is evident and will probably continue. Mormons are likely to move in a Republican direction, as they are seen as an increasingly conservative force in religious life. (See Appendix, Table 16.)

Among the smaller groups, Christian Scientists and Quakers tend to be Republicans, though Quakers are generally liberal on most socioeconomic questions. Eastern Orthodox, Church of Christ, and Disciples of Christ are predominantly Democratic. Some of the smaller churches represented in the present Congress are the following: Apostolic Christian, Bible Church, Church of God, Evangelical Covenant, Evangelical Free, Reformed, Schwenkfelder, Seventh-day Adventists, Seventh Day Baptist, and United Brethren in Christ.

Geographically, Congressional religion reflects the geographical patterns of the churches, as might be expected. Most Baptists are from the South and the border states, Lutherans from the Midwest, Roman Catholics from the Northeast and the North Central states, and most Jews and Unitarians from the East or West Coast urban areas. Some interesting patterns show up, both expected and unexpected.

All four Utah senators and representatives are Mormons. Roman Catholics dominate the New Jersey (10 of 15), Massachusetts (10 of 12), and Connecticut (4 of 6) House delegations. In Kansas, 4 of 5 House members are Methodists, while 3 of Mississippi's 5 are Baptists. Three of the four members from New Hampshire and New Mexico are Roman Catholics. Seven of North Carolina's 13 are Baptists.

On the other hand, 6 of Virginia's 12-man delegation are Episcopalians, though only 4% of the state belongs to the Episcopal Church. Oddly enough, 3 of Nebraska's 5 are Presbyterians, though few Nebraskans are. Two of Hawaii's 4 belong to the United Church of Christ, though most island residents are Roman Catholics and Buddhists. Heavily Catholic-Lutheran Wisconsin's 10-man delegation includes 4 Episcopalians, a tiny group in that state. There are no Baptist congressmen from Arkansas, and only 1 of 6 in South Carolina and Oklahoma, though Baptists dominate these 3 states.

We can only conclude that the religious affiliation patterns in Congress are more accidental than reflective of the dominant religious group, at least in most states. The crazy-quilt mosaic of American religion is reflected in the Congressional delegations.

One final consideration for this look at religion in Congress concerns the relative conservatism or liberalism of the members. Though these terms are capable of many shades of meaning, they are commonly employed definitions.

Several ideological groups, the liberal Americans for Democratic Action (ADA), the conservative Americans for Constitutional Action (ACA), and the pro-labor Committee on Political Education (COPE), maintain detailed voting records for each session of Congress. I chose to use the ADA ratings for the 94th Congress since they are accurate and detailed. Not only are these ratings up-to-date, but the overall rating given to Congress was almost a perfect draw between liberals and conservatives, the "liberal quotient" being 49.2%.

The breakdown by religion is quite revealing. Jews, Unitarians, "Protestants" (probably a euphemism for no real affiliation), Roman Catholics, and United Church of Christ members were solidly liberal. Episcopalians break even and are the closest to the national average. The most conservative ratings went to Mormons, Baptists, Lutherans, Presbyterians, and Methodists. Whether membership in these churches pushes one toward conservatism or whether the geographic location (South, Midwest, and rural areas) is responsible for the conservative orientation is not discernible without further research. Nevertheless, religious affiliation seems to be somehow related to liberal or conservative voting. (See Appendix, Table 17.)

RELIGIOUS INFLUENCES
ON THE MEMBERS OF CONGRESS

There has not been much research on the voting behavior of the members of Congress by religion. There are also few issues that have a distinctly sectarian concern, for which analysis could be useful. A few studies have been published. A study of "Catholics in the Seventy-ninth Congress," by Edward S. Dunn *(American Catholic Sociological Review,* December 1946), shows that Catholics voted the progressive or liberal stance 83% of the time compared to only 43% for the House as a whole. A similar report by Dale Francis for the 80th Congress *(Commonweal,* Jan. 14, 1949) revealed wide differences among Catholic congressmen but a preponderance of liberal sentiment. Joseph L. Hansknecht, in a master's degree thesis at Catholic University of America 1951, analyzed the voting records of Catholics in the 81st Congress, concluding that over 80% were liberals. A survey by John H. Fenton in *The Catholic Vote* showed that Catholics in the 1958-59 session of Congress were consistently more liberal than non-Catholics on foreign aid, civil rights, and labor questions. This was especially true for Southern Democrat Catholics. There was little difference among Catholic Republicans compared to their non-Catholic colleagues.

I have selected for this brief analysis four issues upon which there has been considerable disagreement among the churches: parochial school aid, immigration reform, abortion law, and prayer amendments. Conservatives and liberals within the primary religious communities differed widely on these issues. Catholics and Protestants generally adopted dissimilar positions. This is reflected in the way in which the denominations' representatives voted on the key issues.

On February 4, 1960, Senator Wayne Morse (D., Oreg.) proposed an amendment to the School Assistance Act of 1960, which would have made $75 million in loans at low interest available to private and parochial schools for school construction. It was defeated 49–37. If we include the paired or announced positions of the senators, the amendment was rejected 54–43. An analysis by religion reveals widespread and durable divisions.

As expected, all Roman Catholics except John F. Kennedy favored the amendment. They would be the primary beneficiaries. Kennedy was an announced Presidential candidate then, and he had opposed any public aid to parochial schools. All Lutheran and United Church of Christ members, and 3 of the 4 Unitarians favored the amendment. The United Church of Christ unanimity is quite surprising, as they have no private schools and are not notably pro-Catholic. Presbyterians divided 5-4 against the amendment. Mormons and Disciples of Christ were solidly against. The main opposition stemmed from Methodists (88%), Baptists (86%), and Episcopalians (70%), all three of whose leadership had generally opposed parochial school aid. Baptists and Methodists were especially vigorous in their opposition.

Revision of America's immigration laws does not seem on the surface to have much of a religious connotation but it does. Roman Catholics, Jews, Lutherans, and Eastern Orthodox are overwhelmingly descended from the 50 million European immigrants who came to these shores since 1820. Their leadership strongly supported open immigration and rejected as bigoted the immigration restrictionism passed by Congress in the early 1920's. Many Protestants, on the other hand, supported moves to cut off immigration, especially from Catholic and Jewish parts of Europe. They supported the national origins system established in 1924, and based on the number of immigrants in the United States in the 1890 census. This census did not reflect the enormous influx from Eastern and Southern Europe after 1890. Much of this attitude was found among the indigenous and Anglo-Saxon–based Protestants in the Methodist, Baptist, and Disciples tradition. Few of their members were immigrants or descendants of immigrants after 1850.

Lawrence B. Davis maintains in his *Immigrants, Baptists, and the Protestant Mind in America* that Protestants, after supporting open immigration before 1880, feared that the Roman Catholic Church was using liberal immigration laws as an instrument of political policy to achieve cultural dominance. Protestants had also grown disillusioned by their inability to convert a significant number of the Catholic immigrants. Baptists tended to be the most sympathetic to this viewpoint.

In 1965 Congress finally approved a long-delayed revision of the immigration laws, which eliminated the national origins quota system and its implication of inherent superiority for Northern Europeans. President Kennedy was unable to pass this measure which was dear to his heart. (John F. Kennedy wrote a book, *A Nation of Immigrants,* published posthumously, to promote the change.) President Lyndon B. Johnson gave strong support to a bill generally regarded as a fair, equitable, and progressive piece of legislation. It passed the House on August 25, 1965, by 318 to 95 and the Senate on September 22 by 76 to 18. The overwhelming vote totaled 394 to 113, or 78%–22%. The breakdown by religion is astounding.

Every Lutheran, Unitarian, and Jewish member of Congress voted for the bill. Roman Catholics voted 100-3 (97%) for it, while United Church of Christ members voted 88% and Episcopalians 86% in favor of it. Presbyterians and Methodists were less likely than average to favor the reform, Presbyterians 70% and Methodists 62%. Baptists were the only major religious group to oppose the measure, doing so by 60%–40%. Baptists were almost three times more likely than other groups to reject a nondiscriminatory immigration law.

The hotly contested abortion law issue is certain to surface again and again in Congress during the next decade. Though several restrictive antiabortion amendments to the U.S. Constitution have been proposed since 1973, none has yet reached a floor vote. One key vote, revealing perhaps a general orientation toward abortion, was taken in the U.S. Senate on April 10, 1975. Senator Dewey Bartlett (R.,Okla.) proposed an amendment to bar use of Social Security funds covering Medicaid to pay for abortions. Senator Jacob Javits (R.,N.Y.) moved to table the amendment and his motion carried 54–36. Several observers believe that this accurately reflects senatorial sentiment on possible amendments to overrule the U.S. Supreme Court's abortion decision of January 22,

1973. It is considered unlikely that a majority could ever be mustered for such an amendment and highly unlikely that a two-thirds vote could ever be achieved.

Members of almost all religious traditions voted to kill the Bartlett Amendment. United Church of Christ members voted 4 to 1, Unitarians 3 to 1, and Jews 2 to 1 against Bartlett. Presbyterians (67%), Episcopalians (64%), and Methodists (60%) cast pro-abortion majorities. The most startling surprise is that Roman Catholic senators rejected their hierarchy's militant antiabortion posture, voting 8 to 7 against Bartlett. Perhaps Catholic members were merely reflecting the *real majority* position among Catholics, which in several national surveys reflects a majority in favor of freedom of choice on abortion. Only Baptists (5 to 3) and Mormons (2 to 1) voted for the antiabortion position. There have been several other abortion votes in the House and Senate, and the religious divisions reflected in the Bartlett vote have been almost identical.

The "prayer amendment" votes of 1966 and 1971 reveal a classical culture-religion dichotomy. The powerful Protestant Establishment churches, who once favored religious exercises in public schools, generally adopted resolutions against a constitutional amendment designed to overrule the Supreme Court's 1962–63 prohibitions on mandatory prayer and Bible readings. But their membership in Congress generally rejected their appeals and cast decisive majorities in the affirmative. Though both amendments failed to obtain the required two-thirds majority (Dirksen passed 49 to 37 in 1966; Wylie, 240 to 162 in 1971), Baptists, Methodists, Presbyterians, Lutherans, and Disciples of Christ members were solidly supportive. Jews, Unitarians, Mormons, United Church of Christ, a slim majority of Roman Catholics, and about half of Episcopalians blocked the proposed constitutional change. Members from some of the smaller churches—Quakers, Christian Scientists, Eastern Orthodox, Adventists, and the Church of Christ—voted 15 to 5 for the amendments.

Republicans were twice as likely to favor prayer amendments as Democrats (84%–42%). Ideological conservatives voted 94% in favor, while only 56% of the moderates and 30% of the liberals supported it. Members from the South (78%) and the Midwest (58%) were the most likely supporters, while those from New England (46%) and the Pacific Coast (30%) were more opposed. (See Appendix, Table 18.)

Religion journalist Louis Cassels was amazed at the disparity between the pronouncements of church leaders and the votes cast by their parishioners in Congress: "Passing resolutions, issuing pronouncements and adopting 'position statements' on public issues is a major preoccupation of America's religious bodies. . . . Actually, their impact on public policy, as a rule, ranges from the very slight to the indiscernible. A classic example of how little Congress is influenced by official pronouncements from national religious bodies can be found in an analysis of the votes cast by members of the House of Representatives on the proposed 'Prayer Amendment' to the U.S. Constitution." (UPI, Jan. 17, 1972.)

Which just goes to show how little Americans "obey" their church hierarchies.

11

Parochiaid as a Political Issue

Government aid to parochial schools has been a political issue in the United States for at least a quarter of a century. It has significantly affected Congressional decisions concerning federal aid to education programs. The dispute itself has roots going back as far as the 1830's when government aid to parochial schools was a major issue in New York State politics, and even resulted in the formation of a short-lived Catholic political party. A number of national surveys have been conducted on this issue since 1952, and in recent years several states have held referendum elections solely on this issue. How have the voters responded? How have different religious and ethnic groups lined up on this issue?

A 1952 Gallup survey showed opposition to parochiaid running 49%–40% with 11% undecided. By 1966 opposition had increased slightly to 50%–38%. The poll revealed that Protestants were almost 2 to 1 in opposition, while Catholics were better than 2 to 1 in favor. Jews strongly opposed it in both surveys and their opposition had increased more heavily than that of other groups between 1952 and 1966. A Louis Harris survey in 1963 indicated opposition to parochiaid by 54%–33%. In this survey, 71% of the Protestants opposed while 67% of the Catholics favored parochiaid. In 1964, a Harris survey again showed opposition, this time 52%–

36%. Catholics favored it 64%–24%, while Protestants opposed it 60%–27%. This survey indicated a slight decline in Catholic support for parochiaid, but a larger decline in Protestant opposition. A Gallup poll survey in 1969, using slightly different terminology, showed opposition increasing to 59%–37%. These nationwide surveys, without exception, show a majority of Americans opposed to what a Detroit newspaper dubbed "parochiaid."

To test the validity of these findings, let us look at states that have held referenda on these questions.

1946: WISCONSIN

Wisconsin voters rejected a parochial school busing referendum in 1946 in almost a straight Protestant vs. Catholic battle. The referendum was defeated 545,475 to 437,817, which remarkably paralleled the Al Smith vote in 1928.

Roman Catholic counties, naturally, were the most likely to favor the amendment. The state's heaviest Roman Catholic counties gave 59.6% in favor of busing. The three heaviest Roman Catholic counties were even stronger, 69.4%. By contrast, the heaviest Lutheran counties gave only 31.1% for the measure. They were about half as likely to favor parochial busing as Catholics. The 4 heaviest Lutheran counties gave the measure only 26.7%. Interestingly, among Lutherans an ethnic factor enters into the picture. German Lutherans were much more likely to favor parochial school aid, just as they were much more likely to vote for Al Smith. German Lutherans were primarily members of the Lutheran Church—Missouri Synod, which maintains parochial schools, and this may have been a major factor. For whatever reason, the German Lutheran counties gave 41% yes compared to only 25% in Scandinavian areas. The

Scandinavian Lutherans are strong public school supporters and are considered somewhat more anti-Catholic than their German brethren.[1]

The Scandinavian Lutheran vote was similar to that of other Protestants. There are 4 counties in the state where neither Catholics nor Lutherans are a majority. These 4 Protestant counties, Green, Washburn, Burnett, and Jackson, went overwhelmingly against parochiaid, 75%–25%.

1948: NORTH DAKOTA

In North Dakota in 1948 a referendum was held on "prohibiting the wearing of religious garb by public school teachers." A number of communities in states as varied as Kentucky, Illinois, Ohio, Missouri, and New Mexico had situations in which local public schools in heavily Catholic towns were virtually parochial schools. There were religious insignia on the walls, a heavily sectarian orientation in textbooks and reading material, and frequently members of religious orders, primarily nuns, teaching in religious garb. A number of lawsuits were filed in parts of the country against these so-called "captive" schools. A great deal of interfaith hostility occurred because of them, particularly among Protestant minorities living in these heavily Catholic towns.

The referendum carried 104,133 to 92,771, or 52.9%–47.1%. If we look at the religious orientation, we find that the state's five heaviest Roman Catholic counties voted solidly (69%) against the referendum proposal. A study of 9 heavily Lutheran counties shows that 62% voted yes. Lutheran counties were twice as likely as Catholic counties to vote in favor of the measure. Lutherans are about 35% of the state population and Catholics 28%, so about 37% belong to other Protestant denominations or no church. An extrapolation of the data shows that the other "mostly Protestant" counties voted 60% for the referendum. Catholics were pitted against the rest of the population and lost.

1966 and 1967: NEBRASKA, NEW YORK

In 1966 parochial busing was defeated in Nebraska by about 57%–43%. (For analysis, see 1970 referendum.) New York held a constitutional referendum in 1967, which included a proposal to eliminate the anti-parochiaid Blaine Amendment. This constitutional change was rejected by 73% of the voters. Observers regarded the church-state issue as the main issue, but because there were a number of other questions to be considered in a general constitutional revision, it would be more valid to look at only those states which had a specific referendum on a parochiaid question.

1970: NEBRASKA, MICHIGAN

In 1970, 57% of the voters in Nebraska and Michigan rejected aid to parochial schools. Each state's parochiaid referendum was slightly different. In Nebraska, pro-parochiaid forces sought to add an amendment to the Nebraska constitution that would permit the legislature to make reimbursement grants to parochial schools. In Michigan, however, the state had been gradually increasing various forms of aid to parochial schools until a coalition of anti-parochiaiders, led by education groups, civil liberties groups, and the national organization, Americans United for Separation of Church and State, sought to add an amendment to the Michigan constitution which would prohibit any public aid for parochial schools.

In Michigan, 57% of the voters rejected parochiaid by adding an amendment to the constitution to prohibit aid to nonpublic schools. Parochiaid carried in only 13 of

Michigan's 83 counties. An examination of these 13 counties indicates that 8 are predominantly Roman Catholic, while 4 of the other 5 counties have substantial Catholic minorities. However, of the 5 heaviest counties for parochiaid, only 2 are predominantly Catholic. One county is half Catholic, half Lutheran. The other two are heavily Dutch Reformed. Another significant point is that 11 other predominantly Catholic counties voted against parochiaid. The 19 heaviest Catholic counties, taken as a whole, voted only 51% for parochiaid, or 8% higher than the statewide average.

Of the 70 counties that opposed parochiaid, 11 counties voted over 70% against it. Several of these counties are referred to as "Yankee-Protestant counties" because their original inhabitants came from the New England states and the leading churches are Methodist, United Church of Christ, Baptist, and Disciples of Christ. University counties voted 2 to 1 against parochiaid.

In Nebraska, parochiaid carried in only 11 of the state's 93 counties. Seven of these are predominantly Roman Catholic, while 3 are predominantly Lutheran but have large Catholic minorities. Of Nebraska's 8 predominantly Catholic counties, 7 voted for parochiaid with an aggregate support of 56%. Of the 82 counties that voted against parochiaid, 10 cast majorities of better than 70%. These counties are either Lutheran or Methodist. In none of these counties is there any significant Catholic population.

1972: IDAHO, OREGON, MARYLAND

Only 3 of Idaho's 44 counties voted for parochiaid. Of them 2 are predominantly Catholic, while the third has a majority of Mormons. Of the state's 5 Roman Catholic counties, only 2 voted for parochiaid and only 48% of the aggregate vote favored it.Most of the state's counties are predominantly Mormon. The 6 completely Mormon counties voted 2 to 1 against parochiaid.

Idaho, incidentally, has a rather large number of John Birch Society members and ultraconservatives. In 4 of the state's counties—Fremont, Jefferson, Lemhi, and Madison—the American Party's Presidential candidate, John Schmitz, actually ran ahead of George McGovern! Schmitz piled up 28% in Jefferson County and 17% in Madison County. These counties voted better than 70% against parochiaid. The statewide vote against parochial busing was 57%–43%.

All 36 of Oregon's counties voted against parochiaid and in only 1 county was it even close. In most other counties the margin was quite heavy. The statewide vote against changing the constitution was 61%–39%. Parochiaid ran slightly better in Portland and its suburbs than elsewhere. Oregon has a low percentage of church members and this secular orientation undoubtedly contributed to the defeat of the parochiaid measure. Oregon is also very much a WASP state. It does not have large numbers of minorities or ethnic groups.

In Maryland 55% of the voters opposed a $12 million voucher and auxiliary services plan. In only 2 of the 24 counties did the measure pass. Both are predominantly Catholic. Maryland has a number of solidly Methodist counties. All opposed parochiaid. The 7 strongest Methodist counties opposed parochiaid by margins ranging from 63% to 79%. The Methodist opposition to parochiaid was a major factor in the state's rejection of the proposal.

In western Maryland 3 counties are historically German-American and 55% to 57% of the church members are either Lutheran, Reformed, or Brethren. These counties voted 62%–67% against the measure. The state's banner Republican county, Garrett, which has *never* gone Democratic for President, voted 2 to 1 no.

Precinct data from Montgomery and Baltimore City are quite revealing. In Montgomery County almost every precinct opposed parochiaid, but in 2 particular areas the vote was better than 2 to 1 in opposition. The Jewish vote in Rosemary Hills and south Silver Spring, which went heavily for McGovern for President, went strongly against parochiaid. The conservative Protestant vote in some of the county's rural areas such as Clarksburg and Poolesville, the heaviest precincts in the county for Nixon, also went heavily against parochiaid.

In Baltimore City, Jewish and liberal pro-McGovern areas voted heaviest against parochiaid, as did the majority of blacks. The Jewish precincts opposed parochiaid by about 65%–35%. Black precincts cast 58% against parochiaid but were quite erratic. A number of black ghetto precincts voted for parochiaid, but those in more middle-class areas voted against it. The black turnout was also erratic. Only 36.8% who voted in the Presidential race cast votes on the parochiaid referendum.

The Catholic vote in East Baltimore's Bohemian-Polish enclaves voted 69% for parochiaid, some precincts going up to 77%. An Italian precinct voted 68% in favor. A Catholic middle-class suburb voted about 65% for the measure. The Catholic voter turnout on the referendum exceeded all other groups, perhaps because they felt most directly affected by the measure.

1974: MARYLAND

A "repeat" referendum was held in Maryland in 1974. Pro-parochiaid forces were dealt a heavier defeat than in 1972, as the voters, by 57% to 43% turned down a $10 million parochiaid plan. Parochiaid was defeated by greater margins than before in 17 of the state's 24 jurisdictions while receiving a slightly higher vote in 7 of them. The Greater Baltimore area alone gave parochiaid a slightly higher vote than in 1972 while the Washington, D.C., suburbs voted against parochiaid by a 4% greater margin.

The state's heavily Methodist Eastern Shore counties turned in even heftier majorities than in 1972, with margins ranging from 75% to 83% against the proposal. Some of the more stunning swings against parochiaid came in several western Maryland counties, which historically are mixed religiously but have a predominance of Lutherans. In Washington County, for example, parochiaid was defeated by 78% compared to 67% two years before. In Allegany, Carroll, and Garrett counties, the defeat was 4% to 6% greater than before. The polarization between Catholic and non-Catholic on this issue seems to have increased.

Jewish voters turned in strong majorities against the measure, though the pattern was mixed. The Jewish precincts in Silver Spring increased from 70% to 73% against, while the Jewish ward in Baltimore City declined from 64% to 60%. The more rural Protestant precincts in several counties tended to be heavily against. University students in two precincts also voted against parochiaid. The same majority of 57% was recorded in the Johns Hopkins University precinct in Baltimore, while the University of Maryland precinct increased from 56% to 62% against.

The state's black voters showed the biggest swing against the parochiaid measure. In 2 precincts in Prince Georges County (suburban Washington) opposition increased almost 11%, as 65% of the voters rejected parochiaid. In 9 key black precincts in Baltimore City, opposition increased from 65% to 72%.

Other than Roman Catholic areas the only precincts that showed greater support for parochiaid were several blue-collar Protestant precincts in Baltimore City, where opposition to public school busing had been running high. These precincts, in fact, turned in a much larger increase than the Catholic areas.

1975: WASHINGTON

In 1975 it was Washington State's turn. Forces committed to aiding religiously affiliated schools and colleges successfully convinced the legislators to remove the state's constitutional prohibition on such aid. A referendum was required to ratify the change. The proposal was overwhelmingly rejected, 60.5%–39.5%, a result remarkably paralleling the 1972 vote in neighboring Oregon.

The parochiaid measure was defeated in all of the state's 39 counties, in 7 counties by more than 70% of the voters. In only 5 counties did the margin of victory drop to between 55% and 60%.

The state's 4 urban-suburban counties voted against parochiaid 58%–42%. The small-town and rural counties voted no by 65%–35%. The 3 most heavily Republican counties voted about 65% against the measure, and the 3 heaviest Democratic counties voted 63% no. It appears that voter turnout affected the size of the defeat for the measure. Washington has always had a remarkably vigorous electorate. Of the state's registered voters 55% turned out for this off-year election, which also included other important referendum questions. The 3 counties that had the highest turnout voted 64% against the measure while the three counties having the lowest turnout voted 59% against parochiaid.

Religious influences on the election were minimal. Washington, like Oregon and California, has a low percentage of residents who are church members. About one third of the state's church members are Roman Catholic, but only about 1 in 9 of the state's total population is Roman Catholic. An analysis of the vote shows a modest correlation between Catholic population and the vote in this referendum. Spokane, the state's most heavily Catholic county, gave a higher than average vote in favor of the measure. On the other hand, 2 of the 6 counties that voted heaviest against parochiaid also have large Catholic populations.

1976: MISSOURI

Missouri's August 3, 1976, referendum was the most recent parochiaid test and produced the tenth straight defeat in as many years for the advocates of government aid to nonpublic schools. Missouri, which probably has the strictest constitutional prohibition on government assistance to religion, faced a referendum after Roman Catholic and Missouri Synod Lutheran school patrons gathered enough petitions to force the issue to a vote. The initiative would have amended the Missouri constitution to permit at least $10 million initially in public aid to religious schools. The governor acceded to the requests of the parochiaid lobby and moved the referendum from the November general election to the August primary date.

From the outset observers worried about a Baptist-Catholic clash in a state where religious antagonisms are an established political fact. Both proponents and opponents of Constitutional Amendment Number 7 denied that sectarianism would determine the level of debate or the ultimate outcome. Instinctively, though, Baptists and Catholics, the state's dominant religions, lined up on opposite sides of the fence. The pro-parochiaid campaign was quiet and Catholic newspapers did little more than urge a yes vote. The statewide Baptist paper *Word and Way* gave the issue tremendous prominence, calling it "the most crucial issue of the decade." Baptists and many other Protestants saw the election as a showdown on religious liberty and plunged into the affray with great élan.

The results were decisive. By a 60%–40% margin, voters rejected the constitutional change. The vote was much heavier than anticipated. The pro-parochiaid Fairness in Education executive director Jerome R. Porath accurately forecast 450,000 yes votes but admitted that his group underestimated the volume of opposition feeling.[2]

Once again religious affiliation shaped the voters' response to this issue. More than in any other state, the Missouri electorate divided along religious lines. The two heaviest Catholic counties voted 79% and 72% yes. The four overwhelming Baptist counties said no, with margins ranging from 74% to 82%. The Catholic character of Greater St. Louis and Kansas City resulted in a 50,000-vote majority for the proposition, but the solidly Protestant rural and small-town areas brought down an avalanche of 275,000 votes against the proposal. The county containing the University of Missouri voted 64% no. A "Yankee Protestant" and Republican county voted 4 to 1 no. A German Protestant Republican stronghold voted 68% no, while a banner Democratic county in "Mark Twain country," the only county outside of St. Louis to back George McGovern, voted 64% no.

A survey conducted on election day among 900 voters in Boone County revealed the tremendous religious cleavage. Almost 80% of the Catholics voted yes, while 75% of the Baptists voted no.[3] The survey also found that 14% of the voters were confused by the ballot wording. Apparently 11% who opposed parochiaid voted for the amendment, while 3% who favored it voted no.

Baptist leaders hailed the vote as a reaffirmation of religious liberty. Catholics were disappointed, even angry at the outcome. The *St. Louis Review* (Aug. 6, 1976) claimed that "ignorance and bigotry" were accountable for the defeat of this proposal. It accused opponents of carrying on a "vicious campaign stirring up anti-Catholic bias." Protestant clergymen, it said, "were leaders in fanning the flames of prejudice." The paper ended with a warning for the future: "Victims of prejudice often band together for redress of grievances. Those who made this election into a religious controversy may have sparked such a reaction."

SOME GENERAL CONCLUSIONS

What do these referenda suggest about parochiaid as a political issue? Among other things we can safely say:

1. Religious affiliation is the main determinant of voting on this issue. There is a significant difference between Protestant and Jewish attitudes on the one hand and Roman Catholic opinions on the other.

2. A majority of Americans seem to believe that government aid to parochial schools violates the First Amendment's religious liberty provisions and is undesirable public policy.

3. A significant number of Roman Catholic voters in the states studied opposed parochiaid. There is no demonstrable monolithic Catholic vote on this issue, which may reflect the fact that 71% of all Catholic children now attend public schools.[4]

4. High-income and well-educated areas, e.g., Montgomery County, Maryland, and Oakland County, Michigan, tend to be more opposed to parochiaid than the average statewide vote.

5. Counties containing universities and colleges almost invariably oppose parochiaid by above-average margins.

12

Answers to Ten Questions

We have examined specific ways in which religion has influenced politics. From these data we are now better able to propose answers to the questions I posed in the Introduction.

1. Do individuals tend to vote for their coreligionists?

The influence of religion on personal voting behavior seems more confined to the realm of the subconscious rather than the conscious. A very small percentage of deeply committed religionists tends to cross party lines to vote for a fellow believer. In 1956 a survey in Detroit found 10% of the Catholics switched from party to party to vote for their coreligionists. This was not a significant percentage at the time and has surely declined since then. Religious bloc voting seems to occur among groups that are not well assimilated into the patterns of American culture. Individuals who feel that their religious group is secure are not so likely to vote in a parochial manner. On the other hand members of groups which have been long excluded from political participation will tend to vote for "their own" to even up the score. Jews obviously voted for Abraham Ribicoff in Connecticut in the 1950's and 1960's, since he was the first serious statewide candidate of their faith.

If a coreligionist espouses a political philosophy or identifies with a political party not in favor with the majority of the group, he cannot expect a particularly large crossover vote. In 1956, for example, Jews voted decisively for Catholic Democrat Robert Wagner, New York City's mayor, over Jewish Republican Jacob Javits, though Javits ran about 12% better than Eisenhower.

Obviously, religion has a major effect among people to whom religion is meaningful and for whom religious values are top priority. Religion has little or no influence on decision-making among those for whom religion has only residual or peripheral influence. Since most Americans, including even many churchgoers, tend to compartmentalize private beliefs and public decisions, the majority are surely in the latter category.

Dr. Fuchs defines two basic ways in which religion may affect votes: "When members of any religious group perceive their safety, status or pride as a group to be involved in the fortunes of a political party or candidate, the religious factor is bound to affect votes. Whenever co-religionists perceive their religious values as being tied to the success or failure of a party or candidate, religion influences voting behavior."[1] Most Catholics have always seen the Democratic Party as more attuned to their values, and the specific candidacies of Al Smith and John Kennedy reinforced that sense of loyalty, as did the vitriolic attacks on their religion. Jews saw Franklin D. Roosevelt in that light and have since viewed the Democratic Party with great favor. Evangelical Protestants have regarded the Republicans as their vehicle for a century or more.

It seems, then, that *if all other things are equal,* voters might choose their coreligionists. But in politics that is very rare.

2. Are members of certain religious groups intrinsically conservative or liberal politically, and if so, why?

Richard Scammon warned me that the cause/effect relationship is difficult to determine with reliability. "Does a person choose a liberal religious faith," he asks, "because of his philosophical framework, or is his theological orientation shaped by his denominational commitment?"

Why do so many conservatives in religion also adopt conservative political views? Or conversely, why are religious liberals often political liberals? The answer to this question is not easy to discover, though there are certain philosophical presuppositions that suggest possible answers.

First of all, a basic concept involves the nature of man and the nature and purpose of government. Religious conservatives see man as basically sinful and rebellious against God, at least in his natural state. They also emphasize the personal accountability of each individual for his or her actions. They thus tend to place much less emphasis on the responsibility of society or heredity or environment for the personal actions of mankind. Whether holding the Calvinistic views of total depravity or a more moderate Catholic and Protestant view of sin, religious conservatives believe that man must be changed individually before society can be altered. For this reason they are much less likely to ascribe to the state powers tending toward the improvement of man's natural condition.

Liberals, on the other hand, regard man with more optimism. They have always emphasized education, enlightenment, better housing conditions, better living standards, etc., as a way to produce a better quality of the species. They have traditionally relied upon the state to bring about many of the desired changes in the human condition. Though many liberals like Reinhold Niebuhr emphasized the complexity of bringing justice to a sinful world, most liberals tend to be optimistic regarding both the nature of man and the nature of government. The last decade of turmoil, disillusionment, corruption in government, and a hated foreign war have all tended to make liberals a good deal less optimistic, however, and the views of religious liberals are not so far from the view of religious conservatives as was previously the case. Similarly, many conservatives and evangelicals accept an expanded role for government in bringing about changes in society.

A second factor in explaining the connection between religious and political attitudes relates to the historical experience of the various churches concerning the relationship of church and state. Those who come from established church traditions, for example, Roman Catholic, Episcopalian, Lutheran, are more willing to allow the church to influence society and to espouse a cooperationist view of the role between church and state. In these traditions, the state is often given considerable authority by the church to espouse a certain Christian morality. The state often enforces the church's teachings in the area of marriage, divorce, family relations, and education. A certain emphasis on public morality has been a part of the religious tradition of these groups. There is a modifying factor, however, in the fact that many Lutherans, some Episcopalians, and the Eastern Orthodox churches in general have tended to favor a low profile of religious groups in state affairs. There is a tendency to accept society and the human condition as it is and not a particularly great desire to bring about far-reaching social changes among many in the Lutheran and Orthodox traditions for example. Part of this orientation, of course, stems from the belief that since man is ultimately destined for his eternal and immortal life, life on this earth is not given as high a priority. By the same token, members of these churches generally tended to include all individuals in an amorphous Christian commonwealth concept and were thus less likely to try to compel personal or private morality. Members of this religious configuration were very lukewarm on Prohibition and the abolitionist movement of the nineteenth and the early twentieth centuries.

Many of the middle-of-the-road Protestants—Presbyterians, Methodists, Reformed churches—tended toward the Calvinist idea of separating the functions of church and state but admitting their compatibility of objectives. These groups also gave the church considerable power and authority over personal life and were not reticent about the church's personal involvement in the political and social realm. As nonestablished churches they also tended to favor explicit aspects of public and personal morality enforced by the state. Some of the Calvinists tended even toward an Old Testament concept of the essential union between the civil law and the divinely revealed teaching of the Bible. Many members of these groups were involved in movements for social amelioration.

Another strain of the evangelical Protestant tradition, which is quite different, is the separatist one, typical of Baptists, Mennonites, the Disciples of Christ, and some of the native American Protestant fundamentalist churches. They held a rigorous adherence to the separation of church and state principle and were deeply suspicious of state involvement in most areas of political and social life. They wanted society with a minimum of authority exercised by church or state and tended to emphasize a strongly individualistic religious tradition. By the same token they tended also to support measures designed to ensure public and private morality, supporting Prohibition, censorship of literature and films, and antigambling legislation. These groups, however, tended to deemphasize the direct involvement of the church in politics but emphasized the obligation of Christians to work for a better society. The political involvement pattern of some of the smaller groups has always varied. Mennonites and Brethren churches have generally eschewed direct political involvement while Quakers and Unitarians have always been deeply involved in political and social issues.

Sociologist Lawrence K. Kersten believes that there are at least sixteen major differences between conservative and liberal theology, which have political significance. They give a brief summary of why theological conservatives are so often political conservatives and vice versa.

Theological Liberalism	vs.	*Theological Conservatism*
Nonliteral interpretation of the Bible		Literal interpretation of the Bible
This world orientation, emphasizing social reform		Next world orientation, emphasizing salvation
Events explained by human causes		Events explained as the will of God
Clergymen viewed as ethical and prophetic leaders		Clergymen viewed as spiritual leaders and servants
Stress of intellectual independence		Stress of obedience to authority
Relative or situational standards of morality		Absolute standards of morality
Opposition to harsh methods of punishing deviants		Recommendation of harsh methods of punishing deviants
Changing religious		Nonchanging religious

creeds, doctrines, and beliefs	creeds, doctrines, and beliefs
Positive attitudes toward science	Negative attitudes toward science
Equalitarian role for women	Subservient role for women
Strong ecumenical orientation	Function in terms of religious isolation
Desire for heterogeneous relationships	Strong communal orientation
Social activism	Social quietism, passivity
Tolerant attitudes toward minorities and in granting civil liberties	Intolerant attitudes toward minorities and in granting civil liberties
Stress of group action	Stress of religious individualism
Deemphasis of individual responsibility and support of government welfare	Stress of individual responsibility and opposition to government welfare

Source: Kersten, *The Lutheran Ethic*, pp. 219–220.

3. Do adherents of certain religions tend to vote a certain way when they are members of Congress?

Only on a few, selective issues when traditional religio/cultural values clash would this be true. It can and usually does affect such issues as abortion, prayer and Bible-reading in public schools, and government aid to church-related schools.

4. Do the distinctive tenets of our many religious traditions produce a particular frame of reference within which believers make their political decisions?

Lipset believes that religion affects "political choice in two independent ways, as a source of beliefs and as a determinant of status. And the two variables operate at cross purposes among Protestants. Active membership in a liberal high-status church pulls one towards political liberalism; nominal adherence primarily serves as a source of status and hence strengthens the political conservatism associated with high position. And the opposite pattern operates among the inactive and active adherents of the more fundamentalist low-status groupings."

Jeffrey Hadden's provocative *The Gathering Storm in the Churches* found that America's Protestant clergy were consistently more liberal politically and socially than their congregations. Instead of molding the laity's opinions, however, they were producing a conservative backlash bordering on rebellion. The membership decline in the main-line churches since 1965 may reflect this dichotomy.

5. Is there still substantial prejudice against electing members of certain faiths to public office?

Unfortunately, there is still a great deal of prejudice against the election of adherents of religious minorities to public office. A 1969 Gallup survey found 8% of the electorate opposed to a Catholic or a Jewish President. A May 1976 Louis Harris survey revealed that 20% of Americans even oppose a Jewish vice-presidential candidate. (In the South opposition reaches 33%.) A Catholic vice-president is objected to by 12% of the voters (24% in the South), though a Catholic was named the vice-presidential nominee in 1964, 1968, and 1972.[2]

Richard Scammon believes that a Jew could be elected President but "probably not in the immediate future."

An agnostic or atheist would have a much more difficult time at the polls since even religiously indifferent Americans seem to want their Presidents to have at least a veneer of religion. Scammon cautions: "An individual who was vigorous about his atheism or agnosticism would have a very difficult time being elected. If he were quiet about it, however, and did not express his views militantly, it could be possible, but only possible. It is safer for candidates to have at least some religious commitment."[3]

6. Are there present church-state issues that will likely affect the outcome of elections?

The abortion controversy is certain to remain the most explosive and potentially nasty religiopolitical issue for the foreseeable future. Though many Protestant conservatives oppose abortion and support a constitutional amendment to restrict or legally outlaw the practice, it is the Roman Catholic Church that is most visibly associated with the antiabortion movement. It has reportedly spent substantial sums to influence Congress to adopt an antiabortion (or "human life," as the euphemism has it) amendment to the Constitution. Similar battles are brewing in the state legislatures, and many states that approved liberalization of their abortion laws prior to the Supreme Court's decision were veritable battlegrounds. Church lobbyists placed intense pressure on legislators to adopt or reject the proposals. New York and Florida were among the bloodiest.[4]

Gallup, Harris, and other surveys show that a majority of Catholics are opposed to their church hierarchy's top-priority concern with abortion. The freedom of choice position, which believes each woman should have the legal right to an abortion, consistently wins 55% to 62% support in national surveys, with Catholic support usually in the 50% to 55% range. A majority of Protestants and a large majority of Jews favor this position.

The antiabortion lobby has won no major victories. The various amendments have not reached a full Congressional vote, having been rejected by the House and Senate committees after considerable testimony, including the unprecedented appearance of four U.S. cardinals in 1974. Congressional targets of vengeance by the antiabortionists survived primary challenges from one-issue candidates. Martin Mullen lost almost every county in the 1974 Pennsylvania Democratic primary for governor. Representatives James W. Symington (D.,Mo.) and Don Edwards (D.,Calif.) won landslide triumphs in 1974 primaries. Ellen McCormack's Presidential campaign, partly funded by U.S. taxpayers, laid a giant egg and bombed out even in heavily Catholic areas. Aside from 1972 North Dakota and Michigan referenda, which antiabortionists won, the prospects for a successful antiabortion campaign seem slight.

This does not mean that the issue will not affect elections, because it will in certain areas. A Louis Harris survey in April 1976 found that only 18% of the electorate "could be swung" by the abortion issue, with a slight 3% advantage for the antiabortionists, since they tend to be more fervent and militant in their opinions. Harris concluded that the 3% difference is "not a significant figure and it means that the political dangers of taking a forthright pro-abortion stand have been considerably exaggerated by both the media and the politicians themselves."[5]

Another substantiating survey was conducted in 1975 by the De Vries Associates for the National Committee for a Human Life Amendment. In this survey 70% of the Catholics, 73% of the Protestants, and 91% of the Jews felt that abortion should be permitted for a variety of reasons. Only 5.1% of the Catholics, 3.4% of the Protestants, and 2.4% of the Jews ranked abortion as a major political issue, perhaps the most revealing piece of data in the survey.

Unfortunately for Catholic candidates, the De Vries survey found an increase in distrust and fear of the Catholic Church's political involvement. When asked if they agreed or disagreed with the following statement, "The Catholic Church is always trying to tell people how they should vote. It ought to stay out of politics," about one fourth (23.9%) of the respondents "strongly agreed" and 40.4% either strongly or mildly agreed with the statement, compared to only 39.1% who disagreed. Among the Jews, 34.8% "strongly agreed," while 25.3% of the Protestants and 16% of the Catholics registered similar sentiments.

On another question, "I am reluctant to vote for Catholic candidates for political office because they seem to be taking orders from their church," one fourth of the Protestants, 23.5% of the Jews, and even 11.9% of the Catholics agreed.[6]

There is some indication that militant Roman Catholic antiabortionists are going to encourage Catholics to punish the Democratic Party for rejecting an antiabortion amendment in the party platform. Archbishop Joseph L. Bernardin, president of the National Conference of Catholic Bishops, blasted the omission of an antiabortion plank as "morally offensive" and "irresponsible." He urged all bishops and priests "to bring this information to the attention of your people and ask them to take a more active role in the political process."[7]

Even more vicious was an editorial in the *St. Louis Review,* the diocesan weekly, which accused the Democrats of not wanting Catholic support and kicking the Catholics out of the party. "It doesn't make any difference to the Democratic Party what Catholics think," the editorial stated.[8]

The ultraconservative *Brooklyn Tablet* (June 24, 1976)

also warned Carter that he would lose the Presidency unless he wins 70% of the Catholic vote. The author of the piece, Jim Miller, suggested that Carter "must choose a Catholic running mate." He asserted that "Carter makes people nervous, especially those who are Catholics" because he has "a whole cultural style and delivery that is foreign to people who are not rural, southern fundamentalists." "Why should Catholics risk voting for Carter," Miller asked, "when Ford is a known factor who does not threaten them culturally?"

7. Does the resurgence of evangelicalism in politics presage a new era of political conflict on religious lines?

The New Evangelicals are too politically sophisticated to seek to impose their morality on others. There is also an increasing pluralism within the evangelical community, as evidenced by Evangelicals for McGovern, the newspapers *Sojourners* and *Right On*, and the Christian World Liberation Front in Berkeley, all of which espouse political and social liberalism. The *National Courier*, a charismatic-evangelical biweekly newspaper, declared in its June 25, 1976 issue that "this newspaper does not equate evangelical Christianity with conservative political dogma."

One interesting question being debated in evangelical circles is whether Christians should vote only for Christians (as if there were a litmus test to determine the theological commitment of prospective candidates). Evangelist Billy Graham told a Dallas news conference that Christians should consider each candidate's religious beliefs because beliefs "determine to a great extent . . . actions and character."[9] *Christianity Today* disagreed. "Christians should not automatically vote for Christians because they are Christians," the evangelical fortnightly editorialized in its June 18, 1976 issue. However, the journal's editors reminded readers that an evangelical mystique has always pervaded American life. "Although evangelicals in the United States in the current campaign ought not simply to support those of like faith, there is a religious qualification in the electoral process that is too dear to yield. Something of an evangelical ethos has always pervaded American life. Not only theism but a basic biblical orientation undergirds most of our institutions. Christians have the right to expect that political candidates, whatever their personal religious convictions, will respect the perpetuation of that ethos."

Another cautious view was expressed by the *United Methodist Reporter* (May 28, 1976), which averred, "We believe a person's religion should embrace all of life, including the political arena." At the same time, "it is appropriate to be skeptical when political candidates begin describing how religious they are. From our nation's recent past, we have sad memories of political figures using religion as 'window dressing,' and mouthing deep faith publicly while engaging in activities which run counter to the ethical principles of any religion."

8. To what extent does religion interact with other variables, such as social status, geographical location, and ethnicity?

There is an unquestionable interaction between religion and other variables that may reinforce or modify one another.

9. Will religion ever again determine the outcome of an American Presidential election?

It is possible though unlikely that religion, however defined, or religious affiliation will determine the outcome by itself. Religion will continue to play an important role in the political process and may affect the result of a close election.

10. Will the evangelicals vote as a bloc to support one of their own for President?

Carter's support in the evangelical community was symbolized by three events in the summer of 1976. In late June, Logos International brought out an adulatory biography of Carter by two evangelical newsmen, Howard Norton and Bob Slosser. In *The Miracle of Jimmy Carter,* they suggest that this election may be one "that could bring a spiritual revival to the United States and its government."

In July, Citizens for Carter, an independent political action committee of Christians for American Renewal, asked in full-page advertisements, "Does a dedicated evangelical belong in the White House?" The New York-based group believed that the 1976 election would offer a unique opportunity for evangelicals to support good government.[10]

In September, Harper & Row published another laudatory look at Carter, *The Man from Plains,* by the distinguished *Christianity Today* editor, David Kucharsky.

The analysis of the vote in the 1976 election, which is the real answer to question 10, will be found in the Epilogue of this book.

Epilogue: How Carter Won

Sectarian attacks on Jimmy Carter intensified throughout August and September 1976. Rev. Andrew Greeley claimed in late August that Catholics "should be afraid of the Carter-Mondale ticket." "Carter represents the old tradition of Southern populism, which was fundamentally and often viciously anti-Catholic," he said. Greeley contended that Catholics have now been excluded from the Democratic Party and that Carter's "absolute refusal to say a single good word about Catholic schools . . . has about it the smell of hard-backed bigotry." He concluded that "a country presided over by Jimmy Carter and Walter Mondale . . . would be a very difficult country for the Catholic Church and the Catholic people."[1]

Carter's Southern Baptist affiliation continued to elicit criticism. *America* claimed in July that "a strain of rather unpleasant anti-Catholicism has run through too many Southern Baptists in the past for it to be simply forgotten."

Jim Squires offered these comments: "Since Jews don't believe in Jesus Christ as the Saviour and Carter believes the Southern Baptist doctrine, it necessarily follows that Carter believes Jews are going to hell." He then suggested that Carter's Jewish staff members resign. "Being a Southern Baptist . . . appears to hold more

181

potential trouble for Carter among Democratic voters than anything else he could be."[2]

Many Catholic leaders continued to attack the Democrats on the abortion issue. Archbishop Joseph L. Bernardin, president of the National Conference of Catholic Bishops, hailed the Republican platform plank on abortion as "a timely and important recognition of the value of life" and publicly commended President Ford after a high-level White House meeting in September.[3] The Catholic bishops were viewed as so pro-Ford that they were forced to issue another public statement, assuring voters of their neutrality.[4] Mary McGrory amusingly commented: "The Catholic bishops endorsed Gerald Ford and they may have done Jimmy Carter a favor. . . . If Americans had reservations about religion and Jimmy Carter, they may have more about Gerald Ford and religion before it's all over."[5]

The Milwaukee archdiocese distributed 140,000 pamphlets on Sunday, September 12, 1976, telling parishioners, "No Christian, with good conscience, may vote for any man or woman who is willing to compromise issues which are contrary to the laws of God."[6]

President Ford's campaign clearly emphasized the Catholic vote.[7] An aide told *Newsweek:* "It won't be just abortion. The cultural combativeness between Baptists and Catholics will be exploited."[8]

Many Catholics cried foul. The highly respected journal *Commonweal* commented, "To deal with this one issue (abortion) as if it were *the* Catholic issue—the 'price' of the 'Catholic vote'—is an insult."[9] Robert E. Burns, editor of *U.S. Catholic,* said in the July issue, "Catholics, like those of other religions, will vote their convictions along a broad range of issues."

Two primaries in September suggested that religious prejudice and provincialism may be fading. The Democratic primary for U.S. Senator from New York pitted former Ambassador Daniel Moynihan, a moderately liberal Catholic, against Representative Bella Abzug, a very liberal Jew. According to a *New York Times*/CBS News Survey, Moynihan received more Jewish votes than Abzug in his successful encounter. Ms. Abzug ran best among Protestants.

In Arizona's Republican primary battle for U.S. Senator, two conservatives, Congressman Sam Steiger, a Jew, and John Conlan, a militant fundamentalist Protestant, fought an intense and divisive duel. Conlan is a leading theoretician of far-right religiopolitical causes. (Oddly enough, he is an ex-Catholic married to an ex-nun.)

Conlan, who reportedly raised or allowed his supporters to raise the Jewish affiliation of his opponent, lost 52.5% to 47.5%. Arizona Republican patriarch Barry Goldwater, whose grandfather was Jewish, broke a long-standing tradition of intraparty neutrality to endorse Steiger. Observers attribute the Goldwater endorsement to his revulsion at the apparent use of religious bigotry by Conlan supporters.

Conlan had been stirring political waves by attempting to form a nationwide political party for "true Christians" only. How such a theological litmus test would be administered is anybody's guess, though all but certain kinds of fundamentalist Protestants would probably be excluded. Conlan urged that churches become intimately involved in politics right down to the precinct level. He attempted, through the Christian Freedom Foundation, to politicize Sunday school and adult Bible classes in many churches.[10]

The Texas *Baptist Standard* (Aug. 4, 1976) denounced the Conlan plan and undoubtedly spoke for most Americans: "We want no part of a Christian Party. The Christian influence will be brought to bear through one of the two established parties. Those quick to mix Christianity with the purely political are doing a disservice to religion."

As the Presidential campaign headed toward its conclusion, media obsession with trivial and ersatz issues dominated the political dialogue. Jimmy Carter's ill-fated *Playboy* interview seemed a disastrous blow to his hopes of capturing a substantial evangelical vote. His candid observations on adultery angered many voters, and several leading evangelicals, including *Christianity Today*'s Harold Lindsell. Several public opinion surveys, however, indicated that less than 10% of the voters were sufficiently disturbed to vote against Carter because of opinions expressed in the article.

One prominent religious leader, nevertheless, did explode in indignation. The pastor of the world's largest Baptist congregation, Rev. W. A. Criswell of Dallas, denounced Jimmy Carter and endorsed Gerald Ford during a "sermon" on October 10. Before an audience of 6,000 worshipers, conveniently including a smiling President Ford, Criswell denounced the *Playboy* interview, claimed that Ford had refused a similar interview, and accused Carter of wanting to tax church property and thus destroy America's churches. (Carter had indicated general support for taxing church-owned commercial property in an interview with *Liberty* magazine, Sept./Oct. 1976.) A cheering, amen-calling audience obviously agreed with the Criswell endorsement of Ford. Criswell claimed that Ford would "boldly and courageously interdict any movement" to tax churches, though the President has no responsibility whatsoever in local and state property matters. This was Criswell's first plunge into national politics since 1960, when he preached one sermon after another warning of John Kennedy's election. President Ford was obviously elated and his advisers hoped that the Criswell endorsement would swing Texas to the G.O.P.[11]

Carter was also dogged repeatedly by antiabortion

supporters, who greeted him with angry placards and verbal denunciations in Scranton, Philadelphia, Chicago, and elsewhere. Catholic Church officials in Philadelphia and Indianapolis refused Carter the use of church-owned property for political appearances.

Rightist politico-religious attacks on Carter reached a fever pitch when *The Thunderbolt,* an anti-Semitic monthly published in Marietta, Georgia, claimed that Carter was the illegitimate son of Joseph P. Kennedy and Gloria Swanson! Conservative journalist Jeffrey St. John accused Carter of exploiting his religion for political purposes. "Our traditional separation of the powers and functions of church and state are in jeopardy because of one politician's manipulations in his crusade for a new political priesthood," wrote St. John in his *Jimmy Carter's Betrayal of the South* (Green Hill Publishers, 1976, p. 143).

Religious issues continued unabated, though in somewhat muted tones, during October. Many who fought John Kennedy in 1960 turned their ire toward Governor Carter in 1976. A number of fundamentalist and independent Baptist preachers called a press conference in Washington, D.C., on October 19 to accuse Governor Carter's organization of "efforts to squelch a preacher in the pulpit." Dr. Jerry Falwell, pastor of the 15,000-member Thomas Road Baptist Church in Lynchburg, Virginia, and speaker on the weekly Old Time Gospel Hour television program, charged that the Carter campaign had tried to "intimidate and threaten" the 260 stations that air his program. Falwell indicated that a program scheduled for late October attacked Jimmy Carter's *Playboy* interview, and that Carter campaign operatives in several states were calling for equal time to respond to the attack. The press conference can only have been calculated to embarrass the Carter campaign. Among the individuals appearing at the press conference was Dr. John R. Rice, editor of the *Sword of the Lord,* a fundamentalist newspaper in Tennessee, which was particularly scurrilous in its attacks on John Kennedy in 1960.[12]

President Ford's campaign committee bought full-page ads in many Catholic newspapers which ran the last two weeks before Election Day. One ad addressed the abortion issue. A more aggressive one dealt with parochial school aid. This ad said, in part: "To get aid for private and parochial schools will take a few more people like President Ford. Millions of Americans know that if there were more members of Congress who thought the way President Ford does, the prospect of aid to private and parochial schools would be even brighter. But they also know that having a President who shares their views is a big plus which they don't want to lose." Carter's position on taxation of church properties, the Ford ad said, "would place an undue financial hardship on already hard-pressed church-sponsored institutions."

The President Ford Committee used Carter's religion in an attempt to swing evangelical votes away from the Georgian. In October the Ford operatives reportedly sent 2 to 3 million rural residents copies of a caustic 4-page newspaper called *Heartland: Presidential Campaign Issues of Major Concern to All Americans.* The front page showed a cartoon depicting Carter at the pulpit, Bible in one hand and *Playboy* in the other. Rev. Mr. Criswell's attack was page-one news. Other articles tried to portray Carter as a religious hypocrite, cast aspersions on his claim of frequent prayer, and warned that he intended to tax church property. President Ford, on the other hand, was presented as "a quietly religious man [who] relies heavily on the words of Holy Scripture as he pursues the most important job in the world."

Senator Robert Dole, Ford's controversial running mate, hammered at abortion and school prayer in Lafayette and Baton Rouge, Louisiana. *Newsweek* (Nov. 1, 1976) predicted that unhappy Catholic voters were swinging to the Ford-Dole ticket in large numbers. It was Dole, in fact, who introduced the issue of church tax exemption in an October speech in Bridgeport, Connecticut. He claimed that Carter "wants to impose taxes on church-owned hospitals, schools, senior citizen homes, and orphanages." Even in the Smith and Kennedy campaigns, high Republican officials never explicitly used religion in this way to sway the electorate.

The Republican platform made a direct appeal to Catholic and conservative Protestant votes as never before. The party endorsed constitutional amendments to ban abortion and restore religious exercises to public schools. The G.O.P. endorsed tax credits for parents of parochial elementary and secondary schools. All three positions ran counter to U.S. Supreme Court decisions, a majority of whose present membership were nominated by Republican Presidents.

The Democratic platform rejected an antiabortion amendment, supported only "constitutionally acceptable aid to private schools," and remained silent on prayer in public schools. The lines were sharply drawn. All four national candidates endorsed their respective party platform positions on these church-state issues. Senator Robert Dole had used the issue of abortion in his race for the Senate in Kansas to win voters strongly opposed to its legalization.

Attacks on Carter by fellow evangelicals were widespread. Dr. G. Archer Weniger claimed that Carter "rejects the infallibility of the Bible" and "learned his views on morals from a left-wing rock singer." In the same article, "Jimmy Carter and the Evangelical Conscience" (*Christian News*, Oct. 18, 1976), Weniger urged that Carter be defeated because

> the Carter organization was riddled with homosexuals; Carter favored abortion, opposed Georgia's Sunday ban

on liquor sales, terminated Lester Maddox's daily prayer services, was surrounded by leftists, enjoyed the music of Bob Dylan, and dared to read such "radical" and unChristian theologians as Tillich, Niebuhr, Barth, and Kierkegaard.

Finally, he said that Carter's Illinois campaign manager, Rev. James Wall, of the *Christian Century*, was a "notoriously liberal theological unbeliever."

THE RESULTS

Jimmy Carter's narrow victory over President Ford reveals some fascinating religious realignments. Bluntly, both candidates were modestly successful in raiding the other's historic base. Carter ran considerably better among Protestants than is normal for Democrats, but less well among Catholics and Jews. The CBS News survey gave Carter 46% of the Protestant vote, a gain of 7% over the 1952–1972 average Democratic Presidential vote among Protestants. Among Catholics, Carter's 55% was 6% below par, while his 68% Jewish vote was 11% below the Democratic norm during the same period. Several other national surveys show slightly different results, especially for Jewish voters, but the pattern seems reasonably well established. Carter carried 15 of the 17 heaviest evangelical states, narrowly failing only in Oklahoma and Virginia. His extraordinary showing in southern Illinois, Indiana, and Ohio, and in central and southern Pennsylvania suggests that the Protestant vote was crucial to his election. Catholic defections were offset by Protestant gains in Ohio and Pennsylvania. Carter carried or almost carried several Ohio and Pennsylvania Protestant strongholds lost by Kennedy and Humphrey. Carter won Greater Pittsburgh (Allegheny County) by 25,000; Kennedy had won by 107,000 and Humphrey by 100,000. In Cuyahoga County, Ohio (Greater Cleveland), Carter won by 91,000 compared to Humphrey's 125,000 and Kennedy's 141,000. The fact that Carter *won* Ohio, while Kennedy and Humphrey did not, is due largely to the Protestant vote. Carter's loss of Connecticut (carried by Kennedy and Humphrey), and decline of 10% (compared to Humphrey) in Massachusetts and Rhode Island shows his relative softness among Catholic voters. (Carter won Massachusetts by 400,000 and Rhode Island by 45,000; Humphrey won by 700,000 in Massachusetts and 123,000 in Rhode Island.)

Did Carter's religion help or hurt on balance? In the absence of scientific motivational analysis we cannot know for sure. I am inclined to think it helped a little more than it hurt. A Gallup poll in October found, for example, that 20% of voters were favorably impressed (in a political sense) by Carter's religion, compared to 10% who were unfavorably affected. Seventy percent claimed to ignore the religious factor. His Protestant gains, then, probably outdistanced Catholic and Jewish losses, though the fluctuation and movement varied in each state.

The fact remains, however, that Carter still did better among Jews and Catholics than among Protestants. Both Jews and Catholics are still more politically liberal and Democratically oriented than white Protestants. Lloyd A. Free and Hadley Cantril discovered in *The Political Beliefs of Americans* (Simon & Schuster, Inc., 1968) that Catholics were 8% to 23% more liberal than Protestants on several operational and ideological questions. Even in 1972, George McGovern ran 18% better among Catholics than Protestants. The gap narrowed to 9% or less in 1976 and may continue to do so, but this fact should be kept in mind. A further bit of substantiation comes from a *Washington Post* survey of 1976 convention delegates. Among Republicans, 76% were Protestant, 17% Catholic, and 2% Jewish. Among Democrats, only 48% were

Protestant, compared to 39% Catholic and 8% Jewish. The 1976 Gallup survey on religion showed similar results.

Here's a look at the major religious groups and the 1976 vote.

Catholics

Catholics were the soft underbelly of the Carter-Mondale strategy for reconstructing the Roosevelt coalition. The Democrats were somewhat more successful among other segments of the coalition, but would have surely lost the election without capturing at least a majority of the pivotal Catholic vote. CBS gave Carter 55%–45% of the Catholics, while NBC gave him 56%–41%, and ABC's Louis Harris claimed a dead heat. NBC showed Irish-Catholics 51%–47% for Carter and Italian-Catholics 57%–40% for him. Carter's showing was thus 5% or 6% behind normal. His 10%–15% majority was less than Humphrey's 26% and way behind Kennedy's and Johnson's. He ran a little better than Stevenson and 7% ahead of McGovern.

Andrew Greeley may deserve the political prophet of the year award as his pre-election prediction was right on target. Carter had to carry 55% of the Catholic vote this year to squeeze by Ford. "The difference between an easy victory and a cliffhanger, or the difference between a close defeat and a modest victory is the unrecaptured Catholic voter," Greeley wrote in the *Boston Herald American* (Oct. 31, 1976).

The Catholic bishops' preference for Ford was made clear throughout the election. Bishop Alfred L. Abramowicz virtually insulted Carter at the Polish-American Congress dinner in Chicago on October 10, the same day Rev. Mr. Criswell endorsed Ford. The *Boston Evening Globe*'s headline for October 11 was "Catholic Ire Hits

Carter; Baptists Hail Ford," surely one of the low points of Carter's campaign.

The treatment of Carter in the Catholic press so offended many Catholics that a group calling itself "Catholics for Carter" was formed in Arlington, Virginia, in October. In newspaper ads the organization claimed that "Jimmy Carter's commitment to human rights, dignity and security for all Americans are goals for which many Catholics and the Church in our country have long been fighting." They urged Catholics not to vote solely on the abortion issue. They were rebuked by the Arlington diocese's Bishop Thomas J. Welch, who claimed that abortion was "the overriding issue" in the campaign.[13]

At a Carter rally in Pittsburgh an antiabortion demonstrator held up a lurid sign of dead fetuses with the message "Carter Supports Murder of Unborn Babies." The placard holder told a pro-Carter priest: "You can't vote for Carter. I believe it is a mortal sin [to do so]."[14]

When President Ford visited St. Stanislaus Church in Buffalo the Sunday before Election Day, the local bishop published a pastoral letter reminding the faithful of the importance of abortion as a political issue. Several parish bulletins allegedly endorsed Ford. Several antiabortion state committees endorsed Ford, as did the Ohio Citizens for Educational Freedom, a group lobbying for parochial school aid. The ultraconservative *Wanderer* supported Ford, as it had Nixon over Kennedy in 1960. *Our Sunday Visitor* reported that its poll of readers showed a 61%–33% sweep for the President. *Twin Circle* reported that a prominent Catholic Democrat, Sean Downey, onetime national finance chairman of Citizens for Carter, had switched to Ford because of abortion. Pro-Carter Catholics fought back. A group of 21 Catholic priests endorsed Carter in a full-page ad for the *Macomb Daily* in Mt. Clemens, Michigan, on October 29. Catholic author-columnist Jim Bishop said the bishops had "over-reached themselves." He wrote perceptively, "The bishops were dangling millions of Catholic votes to the candidate who would agree to override the decision of the U.S. Supreme Court [on abortion]."[15] Unfortunately, for Gerald Ford, those votes were a mirage.

It is unlikely that abortion significantly affected the outcome of any election, certainly not the Presidential race. The NBC Election Day survey of voters found a new low—only 26%—supporting an antiabortion amendment. Even in that minority, Carter defeated Ford 52%–48%.

Let us look at the Catholic vote in some detail. Carter recorded impressive gains in several Catholic strongholds. In 29 key Baltimore precincts Carter won a shade under 60%, compared to McGovern's 34%. He carried all but one precinct, while McGovern lost every one of them. In 17 Philadelphia wards, Carter won almost 57% compared to McGovern's 39%. In 10 Chicago wards where McGovern won only 35%, Carter won 50%. (In these Chicago wards, religious influences on voting have always been apparent. In 1972, for example, Catholic Democrat Roman Pucinski carried all ten wards, which McGovern lost, and won a solid 56% of the vote. About one fifth of the Catholics voted for Nixon and Pucinski.) Carter's showing in Baltimore, Philadelphia, and Chicago was about even or slightly better than Humphrey's.

In New York State the pattern was mixed. Carter barely won Albany, but rolled up an impressive 45% on Staten Island—a Republican Catholic stronghold which gave McGovern 26% and Humphrey 36%. (Carter barely won Albany, by 700 votes compared to Humphrey's 28,000 and Kennedy's 30,000.) In Erie County, New York (Greater Buffalo), Carter could only manage a 9,000 majority compared to Humphrey's 82,000. (Carter topped McGovern by 5% to 6% in Buffalo and

Albany.) In Onondaga (Syracuse), Carter lost by 41,000; Humphrey by only 12,000. In several middle- to upper-middle-income districts in Queens, where McGovern won barely 20%, Carter won almost 45%—a showing also exceeding Humphrey's. In the Bay Ridge area of Brooklyn, Carter won 41%, McGovern 23%.

The difference among New York City Catholics might be explained by that famous *New York Daily News* headline: "Ford to New York: Drop Dead."

The nation's 15 heaviest Catholic urban counties gave Carter almost 56%, an increase of 15% over McGovern, but about 6% less than Humphrey. Carter won Jersey City by only 24,000, and lost Manchester, New Hampshire, by 8,000. In 91 small town and rural Catholic bastions Carter swept 55%, a gain of 3% over Humphrey. Since there are non-Catholics in these counties, Carter probably won 65% of the Catholic vote. He carried 6 of the 10 heaviest Catholic states.

Carter swept Hispanic Catholic areas in New Mexico and Texas, piling up impressive majorities in several counties. In southern Louisiana parishes, where Ford was a clear favorite, Carter won 56%—a smashing gain of 26% over McGovern and Humphrey. He just missed Lyndon Johnson's 58%, but understandably ran well behind Kennedy's 78%. In several key German-American counties in Iowa, Wisconsin, Minnesota, Illinois, Indiana, Missouri, and North Dakota, Carter generally ran well ahead of Humphrey and McGovern, winning comfortable majorities in Stearns County, Minnesota, and Dubuque, Iowa.

If the national surveys are correct in showing only 55% or so for Carter, it is likely that suburban Catholics gave a majority for Ford. In 31% Catholic St. Louis County, for example, Carter lost to Ford by 50,000 compared to Humphrey's 15,000 loss and Kennedy's 9,000 victory.

The relative decline in Catholic Democratic vote support in 1976 was probably due to a combination of many factors: distrust that a small-town Southerner could really understand the needs of urban dwellers; traditional Catholic reserve about candidates who emphasize public morality. Many Catholics, in the view of Prof. James M. Powell, felt that Carter's approach to problem-solving places too great an emphasis on subjective factors. Writing in *America* (Oct. 23, 1976), Powell says:

> They can share Governor Carter's deep concern about the need for moral revival, but many stop short at his failure to develop programs and query his practicality. The reason for this is that Catholics are accustomed to living within a highly developed institution, and they expect approaches to reform to be cast in institutional and programmatic terms, while the evangelical Carter regards such approaches as secondary to his main thrust for moral reform, the restoration of goodness.

There is no evidence to substantiate earlier fears that abortion, parochiaid, and anti-Baptist prejudice might significantly influence Catholic voting behavior. The evidence shows incontestably that Carter did well in both Catholic and Baptist areas of New Mexico, Texas, Missouri, Louisiana, and Kentucky.

Jews

The Jewish community apparently gave Jimmy Carter a substantial majority, but one that failed to match the Democratic norm. NBC gave Carter 75%, CBS 68%, but ABC only 54%. The last figure is credible only if one believes that Carter ran 12% behind McGovern among Jews. Sample precinct data belie that. Nevertheless, Jewish support for Carter may have been the poorest, except for McGovern and possibly Truman (who lost 15% or more among Jews to Henry Wallace), among postwar Democratic candidates.

Baltimore's banner Jewish precincts gave Carter 65%, a showing quite above McGovern's 50%, but below Humphrey's 80%. Philadelphia's two predominantly Jewish wards rewarded Carter with 67%, again better than McGovern by 11%, but 7% behind Humphrey. In 5 heavily Jewish wards of Brooklyn and The Bronx, Carter swept 76%, again exceeding McGovern easily and almost equaling Humphrey. In 6 affluent Montgomery County, Maryland, precincts Jewish voters gave Carter 69%, up from McGovern's 62%, but below Humphrey's 74%. (These precincts are more assimilated than those in Baltimore.) In 7 heavily Jewish precincts in Miami Beach, Carter won 76%, an increase of 8% over McGovern.

Five Los Angeles' precincts gave Carter a solid 82%, a gain of 8% over McGovern. These data would suggest at least 75% for Carter among all Jews nationally, unless there was a substantial Ford vote in the heterogeneous suburbs, where Jews have blended in the landscape and vote more like their Republican Gentile neighbors.

Protestants

Protestants of all stripes clearly gave Carter a substantially higher than usual vote for a Democrat. Though much of it was cultural, regional, and economic, some must have been related to his willingness to stand up and be counted religiously. Even in counties not recognizably evangelical or denominationally homogeneous, Carter did quite well.

This was true in upstate New York, far away from any Southern migratory patterns that may have intermingled with religion to give Carter a solid showing in Ohio, Pennsylvania, Illinois, and Indiana. In 13 predominantly Protestant counties, Carter ran better than Kennedy in all and better than Humphrey in all but one. In the 5 heaviest Protestant strongholds, Carter ran 8% to 11% ahead of Kennedy and 5% to 7% better than Humphrey. The total Democratic share of the vote in these historic Republican bailiwicks was: Carter 39.7%; Humphrey 36.7%; Kennedy 32.8%. In some other mostly Protestant counties, Carter almost won an upset. In Orange County, which Kennedy and Humphrey had lost by 17,000, Carter lost by less than 9,000. In Ulster County, Humphrey lost by 14,000, Kennedy by 13,000, and Carter by less than 5,000. Carter made similar gains in 5 Protestant strongholds in Vermont, Maine, and New Hampshire, winning 36% to Kennedy's 22% and Humphrey's 32%. In 7 Iowa WASP counties, Carter carried 6 and won 55% of the vote. None of these counties voted for McGovern, Humphrey, Kennedy, or Stevenson. Carter ran 18% ahead of McGovern and 13% to 14% ahead of Kennedy and Humphrey.

In 6 precincts in Baltimore's 13th Ward live many blue-collar Protestant voters. Rejecting George McGovern 79% to 21%, they gave Jimmy Carter 54%. One third of these white Protestants switched to the man from Plains.

The researchers for the Gallup Opinion Index, in the Introduction to *Religion in America 1976,* made a statement that seems almost prophetic as we examine the 1976 election returns. They said: "Social commentators have expressed surprise that so many people in what they describe as a 'secularized and largely agnostic nation' have supported a devout evangelical Southern Baptist Jimmy Carter. Yet the fact is Americans are extraordinarily religious people. . . . Not only are levels of religious belief and practice extremely high in this country, but an estimated two-thirds of Protestants are evangelicals. Thus the type of religion of Mr. Carter, a 'born again Christian,' sits well with most Protestants and his public professions of personal piety are not found offensive." That is without a doubt one clue to his strong Protestant vote.

"The Evangelicals"

Both *Newsweek* and George Gallup dubbed 1976 the "year of the Evangelical." The Gallup poll revealed that one third of adult Americans, or about 50 million people, have had a "born again" religious conversion. This figure includes 51% of the Protestants and 18% of the Roman Catholics. The political impact of this growing religious force was on the minds of pollsters, politicians, and preachers as Election Day came around.

Jimmy Carter clearly did better among evangelicals than Democratic Presidential candidates normally do, though falling short of a majority. A Wheaton College (sometimes called the evangelical Harvard) poll just before Election Day found students and faculty for Ford by about 67% to 30%. However, since only 10% called themselves Democrats (vs. 50% Republicans and 40% Independents), Carter's showing is quite respectable, indeed about double the McGovern support.

Fifty key evangelical counties gave Carter a whopping 49.4%, a dramatic 20% or so increase over McGovern. Adjusting for nonevangelicals would probably produce a 35% to 40% evangelical vote for Carter. Assuming 40%, which seems reasonable this time, Carter won at least 6.4 million of the 16 million evangelical votes. Ford's 9.6 million, or 3.2 million majority, was not enough to overcome the Catholic, Jewish, other Protestant and nonaffiliated majority for Carter. In addition to his 92% landslide among black voters, who are not included in the white evangelical category, *this was how Carter won.*

The decisiveness of the black vote for Jimmy Carter

may have been partially related to a comfortable feeling among black voters, most of whom are evangelicals, with Mr. Carter's religion. However, there is no real evidence to suggest that black Catholics, for example, voted any differently from black Baptists. In southern Louisiana black parishes, where there are many black Catholic voters, Carter won with incredible 97% or higher majorities. It is true that Carter frequently spoke at black churches and received the support of black ministers in his campaign, but it is likely that this was due to his support for issues which the black community regarded as vital to the survival and prosperity of its people.

To demonstrate: In 1968 Nixon had a 7.2-million-vote majority over Humphrey among evangelicals, which just overcame the 6.7-million lead for Humphrey among Catholics, Jews, and "others." In 1976 Carter dropped to about a 5-million edge over Ford among nonevangelicals, but cut Ford's evangelical majority to only 3.2 million. The result? Almost a 2-million-vote victory and the Presidency for James Earl Carter, Jr.

Carter's stunning evangelical reversal was the decisive factor in his Missouri, Ohio, Tennessee, Kentucky, and Pennsylvania victories, and his near-miss in Oklahoma. In 10 heavily evangelical counties in Missouri, for example, where Kennedy won 38%, Carter won 55%. With this electoral shift, Carter was unbeatable.

Baptists

Jimmy Carter's coreligionists gave him a majority of their votes, the first time since Truman in 1948 that a Democrat won. ABC/Louis Harris claimed a 57% to 43% edge for the Sunday school teacher/deacon/missionary whose religious views provoked so much speculation.

Time called the Baptist vote 56% for Carter. The 96

Baptist strongholds gave Carter an unprecedented 58%, a gain of 33% over McGovern and Humphrey. Carter swept counties that haven't gone Democratic since Franklin Roosevelt. Carter even carried two rock-ribbed Baptist Republican mountain counties that remained loyal to Barry Goldwater and Alfred Landon: Winston County, Alabama, and Fannin County, Georgia. He piled up record votes in East Tennessee, carrying several long-time Republican areas.

(The Baptist press, incidentally, was as impartial in this campaign as the Catholic press in 1960, probably not wanting to be accused of partisanship toward a fellow believer. This contrasted sharply with 1960 and 1928 when, as Beryl F. McClerren discovered, Baptists "used their state newspapers as the main organs of opposition to the presidential candidates of the Catholic faith."[16])

The Religiously Nonaffiliated

CBS News reported that Carter swept the religiously identified "other" and "none" category by 59% to 41%. This group tends to be somewhat more liberal and Democratic than the electorate as a whole. Carter may have lost some potential support among this broad group. Survey after survey throughout the campaign found a few voters volunteering negative comments about Carter's demonstrative religion. A Buffalo factory worker told reporter Finlay Lewis that religion was one of the reasons he was going to vote for Ford. "The fact that he is a Baptist doesn't bother me. What does bother me is the fact that he's pushing his religion."[17] Haynes Johnson found many Southerners chiding Carter for allegedly "overusing" his religion.[18] Some of the more fashionable avant-garde city districts, populated largely by agnostic boulevardiers, gave Carter about the same vote as McGovern, as did several university areas. Nevertheless, he suffered no serious defections, even among those who were put off by his religion.

Lutherans

Carter won an impressive and perhaps unexpected 52% victory in the Lutheran counties, a showing far exceeding McGovern, Humphrey, Kennedy, and Stevenson. Carter ran well ahead of Humphrey in Minnesota and better than Johnson in German Lutheran Sibley County. To a very great extent, the Lutheran farm vote was essential to the Carter upset victory in Wisconsin.

Methodists

Methodists broke even, proving once again their middle-of-the-road status. The heavily Methodist counties in the Midwest and border states gave Carter 50%, one of the best showings for a Democrat in years. Maryland's Eastern Shore, where Carter did well in the May primary, also split 50–50, hardly 100 votes separating the two candidates. It was a photofinish in several Methodist counties.

Mormons

Mormon voters intensified their conservative and increasingly Republican reputation, giving Mr. Ford a solid 65% in Utah and Idaho counties. The Mormon vote may have been decisive in Ford's narrow edge in Nevada.

"Yankee Protestants"

Counties populated by descendants of New England Protestants—Congregationalists, American Baptists,

Methodists, Presbyterians, and similar groups—continued to move in a Democratic direction, away from their historic Republican moorings. These once-solid G.O.P. areas gave Humphrey and McGovern a higher vote percentage than they gave Franklin Roosevelt in 1940 and 1944. However, theological liberalism and Northern disdain for the South did not make them prime targets for a good Carter vote. Nevertheless, Carter won 42%, a gain of 6% over McGovern and 4% over Humphrey.

Dutch Reformed

Carter hardly gained at all among these staid burghers, winning just 26% to Ford's 74%. Carter actually ran behind McGovern in Ottawa County, Michigan, where Ford's almost hometown status prevailed. (Ford had scored over 90% against Reagan in the primary.)

Seventh-day Adventists

The towns of Loma Linda, California, and Keene, Texas, are so heavily Adventist that mail is delivered on Sunday, not Saturday. Ford beat Carter by an 85% landslide. In 1972 Nixon had won 86.4%, so Ford's victory shows the continuing Republican orientation of Seventh-day Adventists.

Carter's remarkable Protestant gains, for whatever reason, offset his smaller Jewish and Catholic defections. Nevertheless, white Protestants are still more likely to vote Republican than other Americans, and that pattern is unlikely to be reversed soon. Political realignments shift only gradually over a number of elections.

RELIGION AND THE 95TH CONGRESS

Catholics maintained their uninterrupted winning streak since 1964, holding 129 seats in the new Congress, a gain of 6. Jews increased from 24 to 27, while many of the major Protestant churches declined. Presbyterians were down 6, the United Church of Christ down 4, Methodists lost 3 members, Episcopalians 2, and Baptists 1. Unitarians had a net loss of 2 members. Lutherans gained 2 and Mormons 1. The Protestant and nonaffiliated categories remained about the same. The only trend of any consequence seemed to be among the small, evangelical bodies, which increased from 13 to 19 members.

The attempt by some conservative evangelical groups to elect only "born again Christians" to Congress did not meet with much success. The leading theoretician of this effort was Bill Bright, director of the Campus Crusade for Christ and a supporter of Ronald Reagan. In his newsletter published by Christians Concerned for More Responsible Citizenship in San Bernardino, California, Rev. Mr. Bright claimed: "The tide of atheism in education, media and government is running strongly against us. This year could well be the last opportunity to restore decency, integrity and a high standard of excellence in government. This can only be done by electing men and women of God to public office, from the local school board to the U.S. Congress and the White House."

Efforts by allied groups were concentrated in at least 30 Congressional districts, where "God-centered citizens" were hard at work to "rebuild" America as a "Christian republic." These groups questioned candidates in detail about their religious beliefs, publicly rated the responses and distributed the evaluations to church members.[19]

The monthly newsletter of Third Century Publishers (*Third Century Report,* Nov. 15, 1976), one of the new right groups which rates Congressional members on the degree of their religious commitment and their positions on issues deemed to have religious connotations, lists 23 House members as recognized Christians. Most are Republicans and conservatives. The organization was particularly pleased with the election of 5 Republicans: Bob Durnan and Bob Badham in California; Dan Quayle and John Meyers in Indiana; and Mickey Edwards in Oklahoma. This group opposed Jimmy Carter and published an "evaluation and rejection" of him, Rus Boehme's *What About Jimmy Carter?* Third Century has also published a book *In the Spirit of '76,* a "Christian's guide" for selecting and electing "God-directed candidates."

Some churchmen vigorously opposed this type of rating system. Denouncing religious bigotry as "alarmingly present in a number of congressional contests" were Episcopal Bishop Paul Moore of New York, Rabbi Marc H. Tanenbaum of the American Jewish Committee, Dr. Arnold L. Olson, former president of the National Association of Evangelicals, and Rev. Joseph O'Hare, editor of *America.*

As I have pointed out in an earlier chapter, there is little evidence of any religious influence on Congressional voting decisions. Paul A. Fisher, in *Twin Circle,* Oct. 3, 1976, discovered as much in his rather ingenious rating of the U.S. Senate: "The United States Senate has 31 members who can be counted on consistently to defend Catholic values and support fair treatment of Catholic citizens and their institutions." However, only 54% of Catholic senators, but 90% of Baptist senators were in this select group! Further evidence can be seen in the voting on the Buckley Amendment on August 5, 1976. This proposal to provide federal aid for parochial and private schools by means of federal income tax deductions was defeated 52 to 37. Catholic senators divided only 7 to 6 for the proposal.

L'ENVOI

It has been suggested that John F. Kennedy was a good deal more liberal than most Catholic voters in 1960, but that his adherence to liberal goals and values gave them a new respectability in the Catholic community. Support for liberal programs increased considerably among Catholics as a result of Kennedy's impetus. Alfred O. Hero's *American Religious Groups View Foreign Policy* (Duke University Press, 1973) charted the swing to the left among Catholics on international questions during the Kennedy Presidency. Similarly, Jimmy Carter seems more liberal, both religiously and politically, than most of his fellow Baptists. It is arguable that his advocacy of liberal policies will help to liberalize the Baptist community. The evolution of this possibility will certainly make the next few years profoundly interesting.

If I may make a prediction, I think that President Carter will defuse the suspicion and fear of his religion by eschewing any high-priestly role. This was never his intention anyway. He will undoubtedly choose a religiously balanced Cabinet and staff and will attempt to worship quietly, as he has always done in his public life. The religious issues that debased the 1976 campaign will in all likelihood vanish before 1980. President Carter will be judged on his stewardship of the Presidency and the results of his policies—not on his religious faith.

Sad to say, religion's influence on American politics has more often been divisive than unifying, more frequently negative than positive. When religion is used as an attempt to win votes, interfaith relations are inevitably strained. It is dangerous and harmful to democracy for political parties to divide the electorate into conscious religious blocs and seek to advance one group at the expense of another. For this reason many are hesitant to see religion explicitly introduced into the political arena. Religion inevitably suffers from too close an identification with transitory, secular political movements.

This does not mean that sincere ethical insights and moral sensitivity should not be applied to the critical problems confronting our republic. On the contrary, they are needed now, perhaps more than ever, to help create a more just and decent society. The abuse of religion and the perversion of religion for political ends, however, are likely to frustrate the search for a creative partnership between religion and government. Nevertheless, religion remains one of the components of voting behavior. It will continue to influence the outcome of elections and to shape the political perception processes of millions of voters.

Appendix

Table 1

RELIGIOUS GROUPS BY REGIONS

	% East	% Midwest	% South	% West
Baptist	12	21	58	9
Episcopal	41	14	22	23
Lutheran	19	55	10	16
Methodist	27	30	28	15
Presbyterian	29	28	25	18
Roman Catholic	41	28	16	15
Jewish	64	10	19	7

Table 2

RELIGIOUS GROUPS IN RURAL AREAS, TOWNS, AND CITIES

	% Rural– Small Town	% in Cities or Suburbs 50,000 to 1 Million Population	% in Cities Over 1,000,000 Population
Baptist	54	35	11
Episcopal	42	40	18
Lutheran	50	35	15
Methodist	58	31	11
Presbyterian	46	35	19
Roman Catholic	30	45	25
Jewish	12	34	54

Appendix

Table 3

INCOME, 1975

	% Over $15,000	% $7,000 to $15,000	% Under $7,000
Episcopal	47	28	25
Jewish	47	25	28
Presbyterian	43	38	19
Lutheran	38	39	23
Roman Catholic	33	35	32
Methodist	31	40	29
Baptist	22	37	41

Table 4

OCCUPATION, 1975

	% Professional-Business	% Clerical-Sales	% Manual Workers	% Farmers
Jewish	46	15	13	0
Episcopal	37	15	22	2
Presbyterian	34	13	30	2
Methodist	23	11	37	2
Lutheran	21	16	36	5
Roman Catholic	20	13	44	2
Baptist	13	7	47	4

NOTE: 17% to 27% are not in the labor force. Thus total percentages will not add up to 100%.

Table 5

EDUCATION, 1975

	% College	% High School	% Grammar
Episcopal	54	36	10
Jewish	54	35	11
Presbyterian	41	51	8
Methodist	27	58	15
Roman Catholic	24	58	18
Lutheran	24	56	20
Baptist	16	57	27

Table 6

PRO-CATHOLIC PRESIDENTIAL VOTING IN 33 SELECTED PRECINCTS

County	State	Precinct	% Stevenson (1956)	% Kennedy (1960)	% Gain
Stark	North Dakota	Dickinson (Ward 6, Precinct 1)	22.4	80.4	58.0
		Wild Rose	45.3	97.6	52.3
		Little Badlands	49.0	96.1	47.1
		Heart River Township	28.3	75.4	47.1
		Gladstone	25.0	70.3	45.3
Putnam	Ohio	Union Township West	19.2	76.7	57.5
		Glandorf	24.2	70.9	46.7
		Fort Jennings	24.5	70.1	45.6
		Miller City	39.4	84.5	45.1
Cedar	Nebraska	Precinct 3	53.5	94.6	41.1
		Precinct 4	50.0	92.5	42.5
Emmons	North Dakota	Marie	15.7	92.6	76.9
		Lake	23.3	98.6	75.3
		Hague	10.7	86.1	75.4
		Exeter	18.5	91.3	72.8

County	State				
Cuming	Nebraska	Monterey	26.1	68.9	42.8
		St. Charles	21.8	64.4	42.6
Fayette	Texas	Black Jack	17.3	56.3	39.0
Dubuque	Iowa	Dodge-Worthington	30.4	74.5	44.1
		New Wine-New Vienna	22.0	65.6	43.6
Stearns	Minnesota	St. Augusta	23.5	66.7	43.2
Dubois	Indiana	Ferdinand—2	38.4	84.3	45.9
Carroll	Iowa	Wheatland—1	48.3	87.3	39.0
Waukesha	Wisconsin	Lac LaBelle	5.6	62.4	56.8
Grant	Wisconsin	Dickeyville	25.0	79.5	54.5
Shawano	Wisconsin	Neopit	30.4	78.9	48.5
Door	Wisconsin	Sturgeon Bay—7	15.0	62.8	47.8
Pepin	Wisconsin	Durand City—1	24.4	70.3	45.9
Morton	North Dakota	Doll	15.9	86.4	70.5
		Dixie	19.7	83.0	63.3
		Carlew	24.5	76.7	52.2
		Little Heart	44.0	91.8	47.8
		McDonald	34.1	82.1	48.0

Table 7

ANTI-CATHOLIC PRESIDENTIAL VOTING IN 22 SELECTED PRECINCTS

County	State	Precinct	% Kennedy (1960)	% Stevenson (1956)	% Loss
McCracken	Kentucky	Milan	30.4	63.3	32.9
		Houckamp	55.0	82.3	27.3
Columbia	Pennsylvania	Conyngham S.W.	61.3	84.8	23.5
		Franklin	23.7	48.1	24.4
Juniata	Pennsylvania	Monroe Township	30.0	49.3	19.3
Roosevelt	New Mexico	Arch	22.0	63.5	41.5
		Dora	29.1	54.9	25.8
		Perry	0	26.3	26.3
		Causey	36.3	58.6	22.3
Hall	Texas	Turkey	66.1	86.1	20.0
Grant	Kentucky	Flat Creek	41.3	61.8	20.5
Dixon	Nebraska	Clark	16.5	33.5	17.0
Caldwell	Kentucky	Princeton—11	52.4	74.6	22.2
Huntingdon	Pennsylvania	Clay Township	28.6	51.6	23.0

		Logan Township	20.9	43.2	22.3
		Dublin Township N.	17.5	38.1	20.6
Marathon	Wisconsin	Stettin—1	24.9	50.5	25.6
Richland	Wisconsin	Richwood	34.9	56.3	21.4
Dane	Wisconsin	Christiana	55.5	76.6	21.1
Lafayette	Wisconsin	Blanchard	59.8	80.2	20.4
Marathon	Wisconsin	Fenwood	9.8	30.2	20.4
Green	Wisconsin	Monroe	29.7	49.4	19.7

NOTE: Stevenson carried 14 precincts in 1956; Kennedy carried 6 in 1960.

Appendix

Table 8

CATHOLIC PRESIDENTIAL VOTING

	Democratic Candidate	1952–1972 % Voting Democratic
1952	Stevenson	55
1956	Stevenson	51
1960	Kennedy	78
1964	Johnson	76
1968	Humphrey	59
1972	McGovern	48

	Democratic Candidate	1928–1948 Estimated % Voting Democratic
1928	Smith	85–90
1932	Roosevelt	85–90
1936	Roosevelt	81
1940	Roosevelt	73
1944	Roosevelt	73
1948	Truman	66

Party Identification (Gallup)

	% Democratic	% Republican	% Independent
1960	57	18	25
1971	52	19	27
1975	52	14	31

NOTE: The Twentieth Century Fund study in 1972 shows 47% Democratic, 38% Independent, and 15% Republican.

Table 9

JEWISH PRESIDENTIAL VOTING, 1928–1972

	Democratic Candidate	% Voting Democratic
1928	Smith	70-75
1932	Roosevelt	80
1936	Roosevelt	85
1940	Roosevelt	95
1944	Roosevelt	92
1948	Truman	65-70 (Wallace 15%)
1952	Stevenson	77
1956	Stevenson	75
1960	Kennedy	82
1964	Johnson	90
1968	Humphrey	83-86
1972	McGovern	66

Party Affiliation (Gallup)

	% Democratic	% Republican	% Independent
1960	66	9	25
1971	63	6	29
1975	59	8	32

NOTE: The Twentieth Century Fund study in 1972 shows 52% Democratic, 38% Independent, and 10% Republican. These researchers also found Jews to be slightly more liberal today than in the 1950's.

Table 10

BAPTIST PRESIDENTIAL VOTING, 1956–1972

	Democratic Candidate	% Voting Democratic
1956	Stevenson	49.9
1960	Kennedy	47.6
1964	Johnson	48.7
1968	Humphrey	24.2 (Nixon 37.5 Wallace 38.3)
1972	McGovern	25.5

Anti-Catholic voting cost Kennedy 2% in 1960 and strong anti–civil rights feeling hurt Johnson among Deep South Baptists. Upper south and border state Baptists went comfortably for Johnson. Humphrey and McGovern were devastated, receiving only 1 Baptist vote in 4. The importance for Carter in 1976 will be the "swing" from 1972 in those states where Baptists constitute a major voting bloc:

	% of Total Population
Alabama	31
Arkansas	26
Georgia	28
Kentucky	26
Mississippi	32
North Carolina	25
Oklahoma	26
South Carolina	28
Tennessee	28
Texas	22

Baptists have been trending Republican since 1960 on the Presidential level. In 1956, Stevenson ran 7% better among Baptists than nationwide but Kennedy ran 2% behind, and Johnson 13% behind their nationwide showing. Humphrey was 19% weaker and McGovern 13% weaker than nationally. There is also a higher percentage of Baptist Republicans in Congress today than in 1961. It is not without significance that the last Democratic winner in these Baptist counties was fellow Baptist Harry Truman in 1948.

Table 11

LUTHERAN PRESIDENTIAL VOTING, 1956–1972

	Democratic Candidate	% Voting Democratic
1956	Stevenson	41.5
1960	Kennedy	42.8
1964	Johnson	58.5
1968	Humphrey	45.2
1972	McGovern	40.8

Some residual anti-Catholicism diminished Kennedy's showing. Humphrey and McGovern were relatively stronger among Lutherans than among other Protestants, due probably to historic isolationist-populist orientation (also characteristic of German Catholics).

Table 12

EVANGELICAL PRESIDENTIAL VOTING, 1956–1972

	Democratic Candidate	% Voting Democratic
1956	Stevenson	42.4
1960	Kennedy	38.9
1964	Johnson	60.3
1968	Humphrey	34.8 (Nixon 50.8 Wallace 14.4)
1972	McGovern	30.5

Many southern Democratic counties are included in these figures and the total nationwide evangelical vote would undoubtedly be more heavily Republican, but these are representative of a large segment of the evangelical community. These voters have also trended Republican somewhat since 1960. These counties were almost barometric in 1956, giving Stevenson an almost identical vote to his nationwide figure. Anti-Catholicism produced an anti-trend of almost 4%, Kennedy running 11% behind his national showing. Johnson ran 1%, Humphrey 8%, and McGovern 8% worse than nationwide. There are nonevangelicals here and the real evangelical vote would probably be 10% to 15% more Republican.

Table 13

POLITICAL AFFILIATION, 1975

	% Democratic	% Republican	% Independent
Baptist	53	18	27
Episcopal	30	33	34
Jewish	59	8	32
Lutheran	30	29	38
Methodist	38	30	30
Presbyterian	30	39	30
Roman Catholic	52	14	31

Table 14

RELIGIOUS AFFILIATIONS IN CONGRESS, 1961–1977

	87th 1961-63	88th 1963-65	89th 1965-67	90th 1967-69	91st 1969-71	92nd 1971-73	93rd 1973-75	94th 1975-77
Baptist	66	63	55	55	52	49	55	57
Christian Science	4	3	3	4	4	5	5	4
Church of Christ	4	4	5	6	6	7	7	4
Disciples of Christ	16	13	12	12	13	14	9	5
Episcopal	66	64	68	67	66	68	66	65
Jewish	12	11	17	18	19	14	15	24
L.D.S. (Mormon)	7	8	10	9	10	10	10	10
Lutheran	22	17	17	13	14	14	16	14
Methodist	95	102	95	95	91	86	84	85
Presbyterian	73	82	75	81	80	83	78	66
Roman Catholic	99	99	109	109	112	113	115	124
Unitarian Universalist	7	10	14	8	6	8	9	13
United Church of Christ	26	25	24	29	29	27	27	24
"Protestant"	20	18	14	11	12	16	19	17

Table 15

RATIO OF RELIGIOUS CONGRESSIONAL REPRESENTATION

	% of Total Population	% of Congress 1975–77	Ratio
Baptist	13.8	10.7	.8
Episcopal	1.6	12.1	7.6
Jewish	3.0	4.5	1.5
L.D.S. (Mormon)	1.5	1.8	1.2
Lutheran	4.3	2.6	.6
Methodist	5.2	15.9	3.1
Presbyterian	2.1	12.3	5.9
Roman Catholic	22.9	23.2	1.0
Unitarian Universalist	.1	2.4	24.0
United Church of Christ	.9	4.5	5.0

The ratio is a measurement of the likelihood of Congressional representation for each religion. Unitarians, for example, are 24 times more likely to sit in Congress than their membership would indicate. Episcopalians are 8 times and Presbyterians 6 times more likely to do so. Baptists and Lutherans fail to attain adequate representation. The nonaffiliated are 38 times less likely to have a member of Congress.

Table 16

RELIGION AND PARTY AFFILIATION

	% Democratic 1961–63	% Democratic 1973–75	% Democratic 1975–77
Baptist	80.0	70.9	77.2
Episcopal	50.7	44.6	55.4
Jewish	83.3	80.0	83.3
L.D.S. (Mormon)	66.7	60.0	50.0
Lutheran	29.4	31.3	42.9
Methodist	61.7	53.6	64.7
Presbyterian	41.2	46.2	51.5
"Protestant"	52.6	57.9	88.2
Roman Catholic	82.8	71.0	79.8
Unitarian Universalist	57.1	66.7	76.9
United Church of Christ	19.2	44.4	58.3

Table 17

"LIBERAL QUOTIENT" BY RELIGION

	% Voting Liberal 94th Congress
Baptist	29.2
Episcopal	47.0
Jewish	76.7
L.D.S. (Mormon)	25.7
Lutheran	32.5
Methodist	36.7
Presbyterian	35.0
"Protestant"	73.9
Roman Catholic	64.7
Unitarian Universalist	74.2
United Church of Christ	65.1
Average for all	49.2

Appendix

Table 18

PRAYER AMENDMENT VOTES

(1966 Dirksen and 1971 Wylie Amendments)

	% Yes
Baptist	72.3
Episcopal	53.6
Jewish	15.4
L.D.S. (Mormon)	28.6
Lutheran	82.8
Methodist	70.9
Presbyterian	70.4
"Protestant" or None	53.1
Roman Catholic	48.6
Unitarian Universalist	30.0
United Church of Christ	43.5
Average for all	59.2

Table 19

RELIGIOUS GROUPS BY COUNTIES

A. The 106 Heaviest Roman Catholic Counties

State	County
Arizona	Greenlee, Santa Cruz
Colorado	Conejos, Costilla
Connecticut	Windham
Illinois	Clinton
Indiana	Dubois
Iowa	Carroll, Dubuque, Howard
Louisiana	Acadia, Ascension, Assumption, Avoyelles, Cameron, Evangeline, Iberia, Jefferson, Jefferson Davis, Lafayette, Lafourche, Plaquemines, St. Bernard, St. Charles, St. James, St. John the Baptist, St. Landry, St. Martin, Terrebonne, Vermilion
Massachusetts	Bristol, Essex, Hampden, Norfolk, Plymouth, Suffolk, Worcester
Minnesota	Benton, Morrison, Red Lake, Scott, Stearns
Missouri	Osage, Perry, St. Genevieve
Montana	Blaine, Rosebud
Nebraska	Butler, Greeley
New Hampshire	Hillsboro
New Jersey	Hudson
New Mexico	Colfax, Guadalupe, Harding, Hidalgo, Mora, Rio Arriba, Sandoval, San Miguel, Santa Fe, Socorro, Taos, Torrance, Valencia
New York	Clinton, Franklin, Onondaga
North Dakota	Emmons, Morton, Rolette, Sioux, Stark
Ohio	Mercer, Putnam
Pennsylvania	Cambria, Elk, Lackawanna, Luzerne
Rhode Island	Bristol, Kent, Providence

State	County
South Dakota	Shannon, Washabaugh
Texas	Brooks, Cameron, Dimmit, Duval, Frio, Hidalgo, Hudspeth, Jeff Davis, La Salle, Lavaca, Maverick, Medina, Presidio, Starr, Webb, Willacy, Zapata, Zavala
Vermont	Grand Isle
Wisconsin	Brown, Iron, Kewaunee, Outagamie

B. The 96 Heaviest Baptist Counties

State	County
Alabama	Blount, Chilton, Clay, Cleburne, Cullman, St. Clair, Winston
Florida	Holmes, Lafayette
Georgia	Banks, Colquitt, Dawson, Dodge, Dooly, Fannin, Forsyth, Franklin, Gilmer, Glascock, Habersham, Haralson, Pulaski, Towns, Union, Wilcox
Kentucky	Ballard, Bell, Butler, Caldwell, Carlisle, Gallatin, Grant, Green, Hart, Knox, Larue, Logan, Mercer, Muhlenberg, Ohio, Owen, Shelby, Spencer, Trigg, Whitley
Louisiana	Grant, La Salle, Union, Winn
Mississippi	Calhoun, Lincoln, Lawrence, Pontotoc, Simpson, Smith, Union, Webster
North Carolina	Alexander, Cherokee, Clay, Cleveland, Graham, Jackson, Macon, Madison, Mitchell, Polk, Rutherford, Swain, Yancey
Oklahoma	Cotton, McClain, Tillman
South Carolina	Cherokee, Lee
Tennessee	Anderson, Claiborne, Grainger, Hancock, Hawkins, Jefferson, Loudon, McMinn, Meigs, Monroe, Polk, Sevier
Texas	Delta, Hall, Hardeman, Haskell, Hood, Schleicher, Stonewall, Throckmorton, Tyler

C. The 34 Heaviest Lutheran Counties

State	County
Iowa	Bremer, Winnebago, Worth
Minnesota	Big Stone, Chippewa, Fillmore, Freeborn, Goodhue, Grant, Jackson, Lac qui Parle, Lincoln, McLeod, Norman, Otter Tail, Pope, Sibley, Swift, Watonwan, Yellow Medicine
Nebraska	Dixon, Thayer
North Dakota	Bottineau, Griggs, Mercer, Nelson, Ransom, Renville, Sargent, Steele, Traill
South Dakota	Deuel, Hamlin
Wisconsin	Trempealeau

D. 50 Selected Evangelical Counties

(No One Denomination Predominates)

State	County
Arkansas	Greene, Jackson, Marion, Mississippi
Illinois	Union
Kentucky	Calloway, Livingston, Marshall, McCracken
Minnesota	Chisago, Kittson
Missouri	Dunklin, Greene, Carter, Reynolds, Texas
Nebraska	Burt
New Mexico	Roosevelt
Ohio	Adams, Ashland, Brown, Coshocton, Holmes, Wayne
Oklahoma	Bryan, Garvin, Harmon, Pushmataha
Pennsylvania	Adams, Bedford, Centre, Columbia, Cumberland, Franklin, Fulton, Greene, Juniata, Lycoming, Mifflin, Monroe, Montour, Perry, Snyder, Union, Wyoming, York
Tennessee	Chester, Crockett, Dyer, Madison

E. Selected Methodist Counties

State	County
Illinois	Pulaski
Kansas	Coffey, Comanche, Jewell, Kiowa, Lane, Ness, Stanton
Maryland	Caroline, Kent, Somerset
Nebraska	Deuel, Hitchcock, Hooker, Perkins
West Virginia	Morgan, Webster

F. Selected Yankee Protestant Counties

State	County
Illinois	Ford
Indiana	Jasper, Lagrange
Iowa	Story
Kansas	Douglas
Maine	Hancock, Lincoln
Massachusetts	Barnstable, Dukes, Nantucket
Michigan	Barry, Osceola
Missouri	Putnam
New Hampshire	Carroll
New York	Essex, Yates
Ohio	Geauga
Oregon	Benton
Pennsylvania	Tioga
South Dakota	Lawrence
Vermont	Lamoille, Orange
Wisconsin	Rock
(Boston	Ward 5)

Notes

1. AMERICA'S RELIGIOUS GROUPS: THEIR GEOGRAPHY AND DEMOGRAPHY

1. *Information Service,* Federal Council of Churches, May 15, 1948.

2. Bernard Lazerwitz, "A Sociological Comparison of Major U.S. Religious Groups," *Journal of the American Statistical Association,* September 1961.

3. Andrew M. Greeley, *Ethnicity, Denomination and Inequality* (Sage Publications, Inc., 1976), pp. 25–26. For a critique, see Edd Doerr, "Religion, Ethnicity and Income," *Church & State,* December 1975.

4. Thomas Sowell, *Race and Economics* (David McKay Co., Inc., 1976).

5. Andrew Hacker, *The New Yorkers* (Mason/Charter, 1975).

6. Seymour Martin Lipset and Everett Ladd, "Religious Affiliation of College Professors," *Chronicle of Higher Education,* Sept. 22, 1975.

Interested readers should also consult Edwin Scott Gaustad, *Historical Atlas of Religion in America* (Harper & Row, Publishers, Inc., 1962), and Martin Marty, *A Nation of Behavers* (The University of Chicago Press, 1976).

2. RELIGION AND THE PRESIDENCY, 1789–1928

1. Berton Dulce and Edward J. Richter, *Religion and the Presidency* (The Macmillan Company, 1962), p. 11.

2. Thomas Jefferson, quoted in Harry Elmer Barnes, *Were the Founding Fathers Pious Angels and Plaster Saints?* (Haldeman-Julius Co., n.d.), pp. 16–17.

3. Edmund Fuller and David E. Green, *God in the White House* (Crown Publishers, Inc., 1968), p. 28.

4. Barnes, *op. cit.,* p. 17.

5. Vincent P. de Santis, "Catholicism and Presidential Elections, 1865–1900,"*Mid-America,* April 1960.

6. *Harper's Weekly,* Oct. 12 and Oct. 26, 1872.

7. See Joseph McCabe, *Seven Infidel U.S. Presidents* (Haldeman-Julius Co., 1927).

8. Fuller and Green, *op. cit.,* p. 137, and Charles R. Williams (ed.), *Diary and Letters of Rutherford Birchard Hayes* (Columbus, Ohio, 1929).

9. Allan Nevins, *Grover Cleveland: A Study in Courage* (Dodd, Mead & Company, Inc., 1933), p. 182.

10. De Santis, *loc. cit.*

11. *Republic,* June 4, 1884.

12. De Santis, *loc. cit.*

13. Washington Gladden, "The Anti-Catholic Crusade," *Century,* March 1894.

14. Humphrey J. Desmond, *The APA Movement* (Washington, 1912), and Donald L. Kinzer, *An Episode in Anti-Catholicism: The American Protective Association* (University of Washington Press, 1964).

15. Harry J. Sievers, "The Catholic Indian School Issue and the Presidential Election of 1892," *Catholic Historical Review,* July 1952.

16. *Ibid.*

17. For an interesting exposition of Bryan's religiopolitical views, see C. Allyn Russell, "William Jennings Bryan, Statesman, Fundamentalist," *Journal of Presbyterian History,* Summer 1975.

18. De Santis, *loc. cit.*

19. Dulce and Richter, *op. cit.,* p. 73.

20. Michael Williams, *The Shadow of the Pope* (Whittlesey House, 1932), pp. 317–318. See also Thomas M. Conroy, "The Ku Klux Klan and the American Clergy," *American Ecclesiastical Review,* January 1924.

21. *The U.S. Government Census of Religious Bodies,* 1916, 1926. *The Official Catholic Directory* for 1928 showed 19.7 million members.

22. Dulce and Richter, *op. cit.,* p. 77.

3. THE AL SMITH CAMPAIGN

1. Edmund A. Moore, *A Catholic Runs for President* (The Ronald Press Co., 1956), p. 21.

2. *Ibid.,* p. 41.

3. *Ibid.,* p. 169.

4. *Ibid.,* p. 189.

5. See Williams, *The Shadow of the Pope,* p. 318.

6. Moore, *op. cit.,* pp. 146, 176.

7. Williams, *op. cit.,* p. 318.

8. Moore, *op. cit.,* p. 186.

9. *Ibid.,* pp. 186–187.

10. *Ibid.*

11. Fuller Warren, *How to Win in Politics* (Tallahassee: Allen Morris, 1949).

12. David Burner, *The Politics of Provincialism* (Alfred A. Knopf, Inc., 1968), p. 205.

13. *Ibid.,* pp. 208–209.

14. Richard Hofstadter, "Could a Protestant Have Beaten Hoover in 1928?" *Reporter,* March 17, 1960.

4. RELIGIOUS FACTORS IN THE 1928 VOTE

1. In the 1960 election, Kennedy ran behind Stevenson in the Dutch Reformed country, in 6 of the 7 Protestant and 2 of the 3 Lutheran counties, indicating the persistence of anti-Catholicism in Iowa.

2. Burner, *The Politics of Provincialism,* pp. 235–243.

3. Two of Smith's closest advisers, Judge Joseph Proskauer and Belle Moskowitz, were Jews.

4. Lawrence H. Fuchs, *The Political Behavior of American Jews* (Free Press, 1956). David Burner, in *The Politics of Provincialism,* discovered that 72% of New York's Jews and 78% of Chicago's voted for Smith.

5. Hofstadter, "Could a Protestant Have Beaten Hoover in 1928?" *Reporter*, March 17, 1960.

6. Moore, *A Catholic Runs for President.*

7. Senator George Norris, quoted in Burner, *op. cit.*, p. 221.

8. *Ibid.*

5. FROM SMITH TO KENNEDY

1. John Cogley, *Catholic America* (The Dial Press, Inc., 1973), pp. 186–187, 188.

2. Arthur M. Schlesinger, Jr., "Relations with the Vatican: Why Not?" *Atlantic Monthly*, January 1952. Paul Blanshard's rejoinder, "One Sided Diplomacy," appeared in the same issue.

3. F. William O'Brien, "General Clark's Nomination as Ambassador to the Vatican: American Reaction," *Catholic Historical Review*, January 1959.

4. New York *Tribune*, Oct. 29, 1951.

5. Boston *Pilot*, Nov. 3, 1951.

6. Boston *Pilot*, Nov. 10, 1951.

7. "Both Sides of the 'Catholic Issue,' " *U.S. News & World Report*, Sept. 26, 1960.

8. Lucy S. Dawidowicz and Leon J. Goldstein, *Politics in a Pluralist Democracy* (Institute of Human Relations Press, 1963).

9. *U.S. News & World Report*, Jan. 25, 1960.

6. THE JOHN F. KENNEDY CAMPAIGN

1. Patricia Barrett, *Religious Liberty and the American Presidency* (Herder & Herder, Inc., 1963), p. 9.

2. "On Questioning Catholic Candidates," *America*, March 7, 1959.

3. "Senator Kennedy's Statement," *Christianity and Crisis*, March 16, 1959.

4. *New York Times*, April 11, 1959.

5. *New York Times*, Feb. 11, 1960.

6. *U.S. News & World Report* May 2, 1960.

7. *New York Herald Tribune*, July 5, 1960.

8. "A Catholic President," *Sign*, July 1960.

9. *New York Times*, Aug. 25, 1960.
10. Barrett, *op. cit.*, pp. 149-152.
11. *New York Herald Tribune*, Sept. 11, 1960.
12. *Newsday*, Sept. 8, 1960.
13. Barrett, *op. cit.*, pp. 160-164.
14. *Ibid.*, pp. 152-160.
15. *Ibid.* pp. 164-166.
16. James A. Michener, *Report of the County Chairman* (Random House, Inc., 1961).
17. Dulce and Richter, *Religion and the Presidency*, p. 196.
18. Barrett, *op. cit.*, p. 29.
19. *Ibid.*, p. 33.
20. Dulce and Richter, *op. cit.*, pp. 216-217.

8. Religion and Politics Since 1961

1. *Washingtonian*, October 1972.
2. Statement submitted to "Religion and the Presidency 76" colloquium at New York Avenue Presbyterian Church, Washington, D.C., January 1976.
3. *Ibid.*
4. "Steer Clear of Politicians Who're Sure of God's Purposes," *Washington Star*, May 2, 1976.
5. "Jimmy Carter's Appeal," *Washington Post*, March 18, 1976.
6. "The Spirit That Moves Jimmy Carter," *Washington Post*, April 1, 1976.
7. "Carter and the God Issue," *Newsweek*, April 5, 1976.
8. *Time*, May 10, 1976.
9. "The Politics of Love," *Nation*, May 8, 1976.
10. Robert S. Alley, *So Help Me God: Religion and the Presidency, Wilson to Nixon* (John Knox Press, 1972), pp. 24-27.

9. Political Profiles of America's Religious Groups

1. Andrew M. Greeley, *Catholic Schools in a Declining Church* (Sheed & Ward, Inc., 1976), p. 40.
2. Samuel Lubell, *The Future of American Politics* (Doubleday & Company, Inc., 1956), p. 83.

3. *Ibid.,* p. 37.

4. *Ibid.,* pp. 225-227.

5. Vincent P. de Santis, "American Catholics and McCarthyism," *Catholic Historical Review,* April 1965.

6. In a June 1976 Gallup poll, Catholic Republicans favored Reagan 51% to 41% over Ford, while Protestant Republicans wanted Ford 2 to 1.

7. Greeley, *Catholic Schools in a Declining Church,* p. 38.

8. Norman H. Nie *et al., The Changing American Voter* (Harvard University Press, 1976), pp. 258-259.

9. *Ibid.,* p. 231. Joan L. Fee also concluded that "neither suburbanization nor economic and educational advancement seems to have had much impact on Catholic loyalty to the Democratic party" (Greeley, *Catholic Schools in a Declining Church,* p. 102).

10. Lawrence H. Fuchs, "The Religious Vote," *Catholic World,* February 1965.

11. Theodore Hesburgh, quoted in Andrew M. Greeley, *The Communal Catholic* (The Seabury Press, Inc., 1976), pp. 68-69.

12. Elizabeth Becker, "Prince Georges Political Leaders Formally Back Governor Brown," *Washington Post,* May 7, 1976.

13. Paul A. Fisher, "The Catholic Vote—A Sleeping Giant," *Triumph,* June 1974.

14. "God in Augusta," *Bangor Daily News,* April 24, 1976.

15. Rabbi Alexander M. Schindler, president of the American Union of Hebrew Congregations, in "Carter and the Jews," *Time,* June 21, 1976.

16. Richard Reeves, "Is Jimmy Carter Good for the Jews?" *New York,* May 24, 1976.

17. Mark R. Levy and Michael S. Kramer, *The Ethnic Factor* (Simon & Schuster, Inc., 1972), p. 21.

18. See Fuchs, *The Political Behavior of American Jews,* and Stephen D. Isaacs, *Jews and American Politics* (Doubleday & Company, Inc., 1974).

19. Samuel Lubell, *The Future While It Happened* (W. W. Norton & Company, Inc., 1973), p. 61.

20. Dave Montgomery, "Sweeping the Baptist Vote," *Dallas Times-Herald,* May 9, 1976.

21. Lawrence Feinberg, "Kin Back Candidates," *Washington Post*, May 14, 1976.

22. Glenn T. Miller, *Religious Liberty in America* (The Westminster Press, 1976), p. 52.

23. Montgomery, *loc. cit.*

24. Religious News Service, May 8, May 29, May 31, 1974.

25. Louis Cassels, *What's the Difference? A Comparison of the Faiths Men Live By* (Doubleday & Company, Inc., 1965), p. 129.

26. See such works as Charles Y. Glock and Rodney Stark, *Christian Beliefs and Anti-Semitism* (Harper & Row, Publishers, Inc., 1966), and *Religion and Society in Tension* (Rand McNally & Company, 1965).

27. *North Carolina Christian Advocate*, April 1, 1976.

28. William Adams Brown, *The Church, Catholic and Protestant* (Charles Scribner's Sons, 1935), p. 302.

29. Lawrence K. Kersten, *The Lutheran Ethic* (Wayne State University Press, 1970), p. 54.

30. *Ibid.*

31. *Ibid.*, pp. 92-93.

32. See Lipset and Ladd, "Religious Affiliation of College Professors," *Chronicle of Higher Education*, Sept. 22, 1975.

33. Cassels, *op. cit.*, p. 99.

34. Mabel Newcomer, *The Big Business Executive* (Columbia University Press, 1955).

35. Edward O. Laumann, "The Social Structure of Religious and Ethno-Religious Groups in a Metropolitan Community," *American Sociological Review*, April 1969.

36. Newcomer, *op. cit.*

37. See Lipset and Ladd, *loc. cit.*

38. John R. Schmidhauser, "The Justices of the Supreme Court," *Midwest Journal of Political Science*, February 1959.

39. Cassels, *op. cit.*, p. 106.

40. Albert J. Menendez, "A Geographical Excursion," *Living Church*, March 16, 1975.

41. Lowell D. Streiker and Gerald S. Strober, *Religion and the New Majority* (Association Press, 1972), p. 155.

42. Seymour Martin Lipset, "Religion and Politics in American History," in Earl Raab (ed.), *Religious Conflict in America* (Doubleday & Company, Inc., Anchor Books, 1964), p. 66.

43. Brown, *The Church, Catholic and Protestant*, p. 303.

44. W. Melvin Adams, "Religious Convictions Form Basis of Objection to Compulsory Unionism," *Church & State*, November 1965.

45. Robert B. Tapp, *Religion Among the Unitarian Universalists* (Seminar Press, Inc., 1973).

46. Dean Kelley, *Why Conservative Churches Are Growing* (Harper & Row, Publishers, Inc., 1972).

47. Constant H. Jacquet, Jr. (ed.), *Yearbook of American and Canadian Churches*, 1976 (Abingdon Press, 1976), pp. 254-255.

48. Press release issued by Bob Jones University, June 1976.

49. See Daniel Yankelovich, *The New Morality* (McGraw-Hill Book Co., Inc., 1974), and Daniel Yankelovich, Inc., *The Changing Values on Campus* (Washington Square Press, 1972).

50. "Opinion on the Campus," *National Review*, June 15, 1971.

11. Parochiaid as a Political Issue

1. Charles H. Anderson contends in *White Protestant Americans* (Prentice-Hall, Inc., 1970) that Swedish Lutherans and Scotch-Irish Presbyterians were prominently identified with nineteenth-century anti-Catholic movements. Al Smith ran poorly in Swedish Lutheran areas of Minnesota and Nebraska. John Kennedy ran behind Adlai Stevenson.

2. James E. Adams, "Warns of Catholic Backlash on Schools," *St. Louis Post-Dispatch*, Aug. 8, 1976.

3. Allison Finn, "Wording Confused Some Voters," *Columbia Missourian*, Aug. 6, 1976.

4. Greeley, *Catholic Schools in a Declining Church.*

12. Answers to Ten Questions

1. Fuchs, "The Religious Vote," *Catholic World*, February 1965.

2. *Chicago Tribune*, May 24, 1976.

3. "Interview with Richard Scammon on Religion and Politics in the 1970's," *Church & State*, May 1973.

4. See Lawrence Lader, *Abortion II: Making the Revolution* (Beacon Press, Inc., 1973).

5. Religious News Service, April 13, 1976.

6. Jim Castelli, "Does the Church Have Political Power?" and "Bagels, Pizza and Apple Pie: Religion and Political Attitude," *Catholic Standard and Times*, April 22, 1976.

7. Marjorie Hyer, "Democrats Hit on Abortion," *Washington Post*, June 25, 1976.

8. "The Democrats Expel Catholics," *St. Louis Review*, June 18, 1976.

9. Religious News Service, June 10, 1976.

10. Religious News Service, July 9, 1976.

EPILOGUE: HOW CARTER WON

1. "Catholics Should Be Fearful of Carter," *Catholic Review*, Aug. 27, 1976.

2. "Carter's Catholic Problem," *Chicago Tribune*, Aug. 9, 1976.

3. Edward Walsh, "Bishops Like Ford's Stand on Abortion," *Washington Post*, Sept. 11, 1976.

4. Philip Shabecoff, "Archbishop Asserts Church Is Neutral in White House Race," *New York Times*, Sept. 17, 1976.

5. "Catholic Bishops Meet the President," *Washington Star*, Sept. 13, 1976.

6. "Catholic Hard Line on Abortion," *Washington Star*, Sept. 19, 1976.

7. James M. Naughton, "Ford Hopes Linked to Catholic Vote," *New York Times*, Sept. 5, 1976.

8. "Courting the Catholics," *Newsweek*, Sept. 20, 1976.

9. "The Catholic Issues," *Commonweal*, Aug. 27, 1976.

10. "Politics from the Pulpit," *Newsweek*, Sept. 6, 1976.

11. Charles Mohr, "Pastor of Largest Baptist Church Hails Ford and Denounces Carter," *New York Times*, Oct. 11, 1976.

12. Religious News Service, Oct. 19, 1976.

13. Michael Kiernan, "Arlington Bishop Criticizes Carter Ad," *Washington Star*, Oct. 7, 1976.

14. Rick Casey, "Abortion Out as Top National Issue," *National Catholic Reporter*, Oct. 1, 1976.

15. "Pulpits and Politics," *Boston Herald American,* Oct. 9, 1976.

16. Beryl F. McClerren, "The Southern Baptist State Newspapers and the Religious Issue During the Presidential Campaigns of 1928 and 1960," unpublished doctoral dissertation, Southern Illinois University, 1963.

17. Finlay Lewis, "Religion Is the X Factor in Election," *Minneapolis Tribune,* Oct. 10, 1976.

18. Haynes Johnson, "Too Much Religion?" *Washington Post,* Oct. 7, 1976.

19. Ray Ruppert, "Religion in Politics," *Seattle Times,* Oct. 30, 1976, and Tom Tiede, "Evangelical Candidates: A New Wave," *Macomb Daily,* Oct. 29, 1976.

Bibliography

Adams, W. Melvin, "Religious Convictions Form Basis of Objection to Compulsory Unionism," *Church & State,* November 1965.

Alley, Robert S., *So Help Me God: Religion and the Presidency, Wilson to Nixon.* John Knox Press, 1972.

Allinsmith, Wesley and Beverly, "Religious Affiliation and Politico-Economic Attitudes," *Public Opinion Quarterly,* 1948.

Anderson, Charles A., *White Protestant Americans.* Prentice-Hall, Inc., 1970.

Andrews, Charles R., "A Catholic President: Pro," *Christian Century,* Oct. 26, 1960.

Anti-Defamation League of B'nai B'rith, "The Religious Issue in the Presidential Campaign," *Facts,* June-July 1960.

Baggaley, Andrew, "Religious Voting in Wisconsin 1928–1960," *American Political Science Review,* March 1962.

Barnes, Harry Elmer, *Were the Founding Fathers Pious Angels and Plaster Saints?* Haldeman-Julius Co., n.d.

Barrett, Patricia, "Religion and the 1960 Presidential Election," *Social Order,* June 1962.

————*Religious Liberty and the American Presidency.* Herder & Herder, Inc., 1963.

Becker, Elizabeth, "Prince Georges Political Leaders Formally Back Governor Brown," *Washington Post,* May 7, 1976.

Bendiner, Robert, "No Popery," *New Statesman,* Sept. 24, 1960.

Bennett, John C., "The Roman Catholic 'Issue' Again," *Christianity and Crisis,* Sept. 19, 1960.

———"A Roman Catholic for President?" *Christianity and Crisis,* March 7, 1960.

———"Triumph for American Democracy," *Christianity and Crisis,* Nov. 28, 1960.

Billington, Ray Allen, *The Protestant Crusade 1800-1860.* The Macmillan Company, 1939.

Bird, Robert S., and Price, Jo-Ann, "All-out Religious Attack on Kennedy Planned by 38 Fundamentalist Sects," *New York Herald Tribune,* Oct. 16, 1960.

Blake, Eugene Carson, and Oxnam, G. Bromley, "A Protestant View of a Catholic for President," *Look,* May 10, 1960.

Blanshard, Paul, *American Freedom and Catholic Power.* Beacon Press, Inc., 1949.

Bonnell, John Sutherland, "Religion and the Presidency," *Presbyterian Life,* May 1, 1960.

Bosley, Harold A., "A Catholic President: Con," *Christian Century,* Oct. 26, 1960.

"Both Sides of the 'Catholic Issue,' " *U.S. News & World Report,* Sept. 26, 1960.

Brenner, Saul, "Patterns of Jewish-Catholic Democratic Voting and the 1960 Presidential Vote," *Jewish Social Studies,* July 1964.

Brown, Harold O. J., "Restive Evangelicals," *National Review,* Feb. 15, 1974.

Burner, David, *The Politics of Provincialism.* Alfred A. Knopf, Inc., 1968.

Burns, James MacGregor, "The Religious Issue," *Progressive,* November 1960.

Canavan, Francis, "Politics and Catholicism," *Social Order,* December 1959.

Carleton, William G., "The Popish Plot of 1928," *Forum,* September 1949.

Carter, Douglas, "The Protestant Issue," *Reporter,* Oct. 13, 1960.

Carter, Paul A., "The Campaign of 1928 Re-examined," *Wisconsin Magazine of History,* Summer 1963.

Cassels, Louis, *What's the Difference? A Comparison of the Faiths Men Live By.* Doubleday & Company, Inc., 1965.

Castelli, Jim, "Does the Church Have Political Power?" *Catholic Standard and Times*, April 22, 1976.

"Catholic Vote: A Kennedy Staff Analysis," *U.S. News & World Report*, Aug. 1, 1960.

"Catholicism and the Campaign," *Commonweal*, Sept. 23, 1960.

Cogley, John, *Catholic America*. The Dial Press, Inc., 1973.

Cohen, Henry, and Sandrow, Gary, *Philadelphia Chooses a Mayor, 1971: Jewish Voting Patterns*. New York: American Jewish Committee, 1972.

Connell, Francis J., "Now That the Election Is Over," *American Ecclesiastical Review*, January 1961.

Conroy, Thomas M., "The Ku Klux Klan and the American Clergy," *American Ecclesiastical Review*, January 1924.

Converse, Phillip E., *Religion and Politics: The 1960 Election*. University of Michigan Survey Research Center, 1961.

Coughlan, Robert, "The Religious Issue: An Un-American Heritage," *Life*, July 4, 1960.

Cour, Raymond F., "Catholics in Public Office," *Commonweal*, Sept. 16, 1960.

Danzig, David, "Bigotry and the Presidency," *Commonweal*, Sept. 23, 1960.

———"The Radical Right and the Rise of the Fundamentalist Minority," *Commentary*, April 1962.

Davis, Lawrence B., *Immigrants, Baptists and the Protestant Mind in America*. University of Illinois Press, 1973.

Dawidowicz, Lucy S., and Goldstein, Leon J., *Politics in a Pluralist Democracy*. Institute of Human Relations Press, 1963.

De Santis, Vincent P., "American Catholics and McCarthyism," *Catholic Historical Review*, April 1965.

———"Catholicism and Presidential Elections, 1865-1900," *Mid-America*, April 1960.

Desmond, Humphrey J., *The APA Movement*. Washington, 1912.

Doerr, Edd, "Religion, Ethnicity and Income," *Church & State*, December 1975.

"Does Religion Influence Voting in America?" *Jewish Forum*, July 1960.

Doherty, Herbert J., "Florida and the Presidential Election of 1928," *Florida Historical Quarterly*, October 1947.

Dugger, Ronnie, "Politicians in the Pulpit," *Texas Observer*, Sept. 30, 1960.

Dulce, Berton, and Richter, Edward J., *Religion and the Presidency.* The Macmillan Company, 1962.

Dunn, Edward S., "Catholics in the Seventy-ninth Congress," *American Catholic Sociological Review*, December 1946.

Feinberg, Lawrence, "Kin Back Candidates," *Washington Post*, May 14, 1976.

Felknor, Bruce L., *Dirty Politics.* W. W. Norton & Company, Inc., 1966.

Fenton, John H., *The Catholic Vote.* Hauser Press, 1960.

Fisher, Paul A., "The Catholic Vote—A Sleeping Giant," *Triumph*, June 1974.

Fuchs, Lawrence H., *The Political Behavior of American Jews.* Free Press, 1956.

———"The Religious Vote," *Catholic World*, February 1965.

———"Religious Vote, Fact or Fiction?" *Catholic World*, October 1960.

Fuller, Edmund, and Green, David E., *God in the White House.* Crown Publishers, Inc., 1968.

Gallup, George, *Religion in America 1971.* Princeton, N.J., 1971.

———*Religion in America 1976.* Princeton, N.J., 1976.

Geantz, Oscar, "Protestant and Catholic Voting in a Metropolitan Area," *Public Opinion Quarterly*, Spring 1959.

Gelman, Norman I., "Religion in Politics," *Editorial Research Reports*, Sept. 9, 1959.

Geylin, Philip, "The Religious Issue: Anti-Catholicism Runs Deeper than Expected, May Backfire on GOP," *Wall Street Journal*, Sept. 12, 1960.

Gladden, Washington, "The Anti-Catholic Crusade," *Century*, March 1894.

———"The Anti-Papal Panic," *Harper's Weekly*, July 18, 1914.

"God in Augusta," *Bangor Daily News*, April 24, 1976.

Gold, David, "The Influence of Religious Affiliation on Voting Behavior." Unpublished doctoral dissertation, University of Chicago, 1953.

Greeley, Andrew M., *Catholic Schools in a Declining Church.* Sheed & Ward, Inc., 1976.

——— *Ethnicity, Denomination and Inequality.* Sage Publications, Inc., 1976.

—— "Religion Figures in U.S. Politics Again," *San Francisco Chronicle,* June 12, 1976.

Guysenir, Maurice, "Jewish Vote in Chicago," *Jewish Social Studies,* October 1958.

Hacker, Andrew, *The New Yorkers.* Mason/Charter, 1975.

Hadden, Jeffrey, *The Gathering Storm in the Churches.* Doubleday & Company, Inc., 1969.

Hardon, John A., "A Catholic in the White House," *Homiletic and Pastoral Review,* September 1960.

Hattery, John W., "The Presidential Election Campaigns of 1928 and 1960: A Comparison of the Christian Century and America," *Journal of Church and State,* Winter 1967.

Hillis, Don W., *If America Elects a Catholic President.* Dunham Publishing Company, 1959.

Hofstadter, Richard, "Could a Protestant Have Beaten Hoover in 1928?" *Reporter,* March 17, 1960.

Howe, Mark DeWolfe, "Diplomacy, Religion and the Constitution," *Nation,* Jan. 12, 1952.

Hoyt, Robert, "Kennedy, Catholicism and the Presidency," *Jubilee,* December 1960.

Hyer, Marjorie, "Democrats Hit on Abortion," *Washington Post,* June 25, 1976.

"An Interview with Richard Scammon on Religion and Politics in the 1970's," *Church & State,* May 1973.

Isaacs, Stephen D., *Jews and American Politics.* Doubleday & Company, Inc., 1974.

Jacquet, Constant H., Jr. (ed.), *Yearbook of American and Canadian Churches, 1976.* Abingdon Press, 1976.

Johnson, Douglas W.; Picard, Paul R.; and Quinn, Bernard, *Churches and Church Membership in the United States, 1971.* Washington, D.C.: Glenmary Research Center, 1974.

Jorstad, Erling, *The Politics of Doomsday.* Abingdon Press, 1970.

Kelley, George, "A Time for Keeping On of Shirts," *America,* Sept. 24, 1960.

Kersten, Lawrence K., *The Lutheran Ethic.* Wayne State University Press, 1970.

Kim, Richard C., "A Roman Catholic President in the American Schema," *Journal of Church and State,* May 1961.

Kinzer, Donald L., *An Episode in Anti-Catholicism: The American Protective Association.* University of Washington Press, 1964.

Knebel, Fletcher, "Democratic Forecast: A Catholic in 1960," *Look*, March 3, 1959.

Lader, Lawrence, *Abortion II: Making the Revolution*. Beacon Press, Inc., 1973.

Laumann, Edward O., "The Social Structure of Religious and Ethno-Religious Groups in a Metropolitan Community," *American Sociological Review*, April 1969.

Lazerwitz, Bernard, "A Sociological Comparison of Major U.S. Religious Groups," *Journal of the American Statistical Association*, September 1961.

Lenski, Gerhard, *The Religious Factor*. Doubleday & Company, Inc., 1961.

Levy, Mark R., and Kramer, Michael S., *The Ethnic Factor*. Simon & Schuster, Inc., 1972.

Lipset, Seymour Martin, "Some Statistics on Bigotry in Voting," *Commentary*, October 1960.

Lipset, Seymour Martin, and Ladd, Everett, "Religious Affiliation of College Professors," *Chronicle of Higher Education*, Sept. 22, 1975.

Lipset, Seymour Martin, and Raab, Earl, *The Politics of Unreason*. Harper & Row, Publishers, Inc., 1970.

Lubell, Samuel, *The Future of American Politics*. Doubleday & Company, Inc., 1956.

——*The Future While It Happened*. W. W. Norton & Company, Inc., 1973.

Lynn, Frank, "Politics Must Take Account of Catholicism," *New York Times*, Nov. 2, 1975.

McAvoy, Thomas T., "Where Is the Catholic Vote?" *Ave Maria*, June 16, 1956.

McCabe, Joseph, *Seven Infidel U.S. Presidents*. Haldeman-Julius Co., 1927.

McClerren, Beryl F., "The Southern Baptist State Newspapers and the Religious Issue During the Presidential Campaigns of 1928 and 1960," Unpublished doctoral dissertation, Southern Illinois University, 1963.

McKinney, Madge W., "Religion and Elections," *Public Opinion Quarterly*, Spring 1944.

McWilliams, Carey, "The Church-State Issue," *Nation*, April 24, 1972.

Marshall, Charles C., *Governor Smith's American Catholicism.* Dodd, Mead & Company, Inc., 1928.

———"An Open Letter to the Honorable Alfred E. Smith," *Atlantic Monthly,* April 1927.

Menendez, Albert J., "A Geographical Excursion," *Living Church,* March 16, 1975.

———"Jimmy Carter: The Religious Issue Revisited," *Humanist,* July/August 1976.

———"Will Evangelicals Swing the Election?" *Christianity Today,* June 18, 1976.

Michener, James A., *Report of the County Chairman.* Random House, Inc., 1961.

Miller, Glenn T., *Religious Liberty in America.* The Westminster Press, 1976.

Miller, Robert M., "A Footnote to the Role of the Protestant Churches in the Election of 1928," *Church History,* June 1956.

——— "A Note on the Relation Between the Protestant Churches and the Revival of the Ku Klux Klan," *Journal of Southern History,* August 1956.

Mims, Forrest M., "The Jimmy Carter Candidacy: Sobering Implications for Southern Baptists?" *Baptist New Mexican,* May 29, 1976.

Montgomery, Dave, "Sweeping the Baptist Vote," *Dallas Times-Herald,* May 9, 1976.

Moore, Arthur, "Protestant Positions on a Catholic in the White House," *Commonweal,* Sept. 30, 1960.

Moore, Edmund A., *A Catholic Runs for President.* The Ronald Press Co., 1956.

Morgan, Richard E., *The Politics of Religious Conflict.* Pegasus, 1968.

Murray, John Courtney, *We Hold These Truths.* Sheed & Ward, Inc., 1960.

Nations, Gilbert O., *The Political Career of Alfred E. Smith.* Washington, D.C.: The Protestant, 1928.

Neusner, Jacob, "Religion and Politics," *Jewish Ledger,* Aug. 4, 1960.

Newcomer, Mabel, *The Big Business Executive.* Columbia University Press, 1955.

Nie, Norman H., *et al.*, *The Changing American Voter.* Harvard University Press, 1976.

Niebuhr, Reinhold, "Catholics and the Presidency," *New Leader*, May 9, 1960.

———"The Religious Issue," *New Leader*, Dec. 12, 1960.

"The 1960 Election Campaign," *Facts*, March 1961.

Norton, Howard, and Slosser, Bob, *The Miracle of Jimmy Carter.* Logos International, 1976.

Novak, Michael, "Can a Protestant Be Nominated?" *Christian Century*, June 20, 1975.

——— "Jewish Agenda, Catholic Agenda," *Commonweal*, June 28, 1974.

O'Brien, F. William, "General Clark's Nomination as Ambassador to the Vatican: American Reaction," *Catholic Historical Review*, January 1959.

Odegard, Peter H. (ed.), *Religion and Politics.* Published for the Eagleton Institute of Politics at Rugers University. Oceana Publications, 1960.

Ogburn, William F., and Talbot, Nell S., "A Measurement of the Factors in the Presidential Election of 1928," *Social Forces*, December 1929.

O'Neill, James M., *Catholicism and American Freedom.* Harper & Brothers, 1952.

"On Raising the Religious Issue: A Symposium," *America*, Sept. 24, 1960.

"Opinion on the Campus," *National Review*, June 15, 1971.

Phillips, Kevin, *The Emerging Republican Majority.* Arlington House, 1969.

Picrard, Richard V., *The Unequal Yoke.* J. B. Lippincott Company, 1970.

Pike, James A., and Byfield, Richard, *A Roman Catholic in the White House.* Doubleday & Company, Inc., 1960.

Raab, Earl (ed.), *Religious Conflict in America.* Doubleday & Company, Inc., Anchor Books, 1964.

Reeves, Richard, "Is Jimmy Carter Good for the Jews?" *New York*, May 24, 1976.

"Religion in the Campaign," *Commonweal*, Aug. 5, 1960.

Roper, Elmo, "The Catholic Vote: A Second Look," *Saturday Review*, Nov. 5, 1960.

———— "The Myth of the Catholic Vote," *Saturday Review*, Oct. 31, 1959.

Rosten, Leo (ed.), *Religions of America: Ferment and Faith in an Age of Crisis, A New Guide and Almanac.* Simon & Schuster, Inc., 1975.

Roy, Ralph Lord, *Apostles of Discord: A Study of Organized Bigotry and Disruption on the Fringes of Protestantism.* Beacon Press, Inc., 1953.

Russell, C. Allyn, "William Jennings Bryan, Statesman, Fundamentalist," *Journal of Presbyterian History*, Summer 1975.

Ryan, John A., "A Catholic View of the Election," *Current History*, December 1928.

Scharper, Philip, "Why Protestants Fear Us," *Ave Maria*, May 28, 1960.

Schauinger, J. Herman, *Profiles in Action: American Catholics in Public Life.* Bruce Publishing Company, 1966.

Schmidhauser, John R., "The Justices of the Supreme Court," *Midwest Journal of Political Science*, February 1959.

Schroeder, Theodore, *Al Smith, the Pope and the Presidency.* New York, 1928.

Shelton, Willard, "The How and Why of Kennedy's Victory," *American Federationist*, December 1960.

Shinn, Roger L., "What the Campaign Did to Religion," *Christianity and Crisis*, Nov. 14, 1960.

Sievers, Harry J., "The Catholic Indian School Issue and the Presidential Election of 1892," *Catholic Historical Review*, July 1952.

Silva, Ruth C., *Rum, Religion and Votes.* Pennsylvania State University Press, 1962.

Simon, P., "Catholicism and the Elections," *Commonweal*, July 22, 1960.

Smith, Alfred E., "Patriot and Catholic," *Atlantic Monthly*, May 1927.

Smith, Rembert Gilman, *Politics in a Protestant Church.* Atlanta, 1930.

Smylie, James H., "The Roman Catholic Church, the State and Al Smith," *Church History*, September 1960.

Sowell, Thomas, *Race and Economics.* David McKay Co., Inc., 1976.

Stange, Douglas C., "Al Smith and the Republican Party at Prayer: The Lutheran Vote—1928," *Review of Politics*, July 1970.

Stedman, Murray S., *Religion and Politics in America*. Harcourt, Brace and World, Inc., 1964.

Sterling, Claire, "The Vatican and Kennedy," *Reporter*, Oct. 27, 1960.

Streiker, Lowell D., and Strober, Gerald S., *Religion and the New Majority*. Association Press, 1972.

Swomley, John M., "Manipulating the Blocs: Church, State and Mr. Nixon," *Nation*, Sept. 11, 1972.

Talley, James, "Ministers See Pulpit Attacks on Kennedy Bid," *Nashville Tennessean*, Aug. 15, 1960.

Tapp, Robert B., *Religion Among the Unitarian Universalists*. Seminar Press, Inc., 1973.

Teller, Judd L., "The Jewish Vote—Myth or Fact?" *Midstream*, Summer 1960.

Vorspan, Albert, "Jewish Voters and the Religious Issue," *Jewish Frontier*, October 1960.

Walker, Brooks R., *The Christian Fright Peddlers*. Doubleday & Company, Inc., 1964.

Warren, Fuller, *How to Win in Politics*. Tallahassee: Allen Morris, 1949.

Watson, Richard A., "Religion and Politics in Mid-America—Presidential Voting in Missouri in 1928 and 1960," *Midcontinent American Studies Journal*, Spring 1964.

Weyl, Nathaniel, *The Jew in American Politics*. Arlington House, 1968.

White, Theodore H., *The Making of the President 1960*. Atheneum Publishers, 1961.

Wicklein, John, "Anti-Catholic Groups Closely Cooperate in Mail Campaign to Defeat Kennedy," *New York Times*, Oct. 17, 1960.

————"Religious Issue Revisited," *American Judaism*, April 1961.

Williams, J. Paul, *What Americans Believe and How They Worship*. Harper & Brothers, 1952.

Williams, Michael, *The Shadow of the Pope*. Whittlesey House, 1932.

Woelfel, LaSalle, "The Oldest American Prejudice," *America*, Sept. 24, 1960.

See also the following articles written during the 1976 Presidential campaign:

Adams, James Luther, "The Fundamentalist for Right Rides Again," *Humanist*, Sept.-Oct. 1976.

Baker, James T., "Jimmy Carter's Religion," *Commonweal*, July 1, 1976.

Birdwhistell, Ira V., "Southern Baptists and Roman Catholics," *Ecumenist*, Vol. 14, No. 4 (May-June 1976).

Boyd, Forrest, "Do We Really Want a Saint in the White House?" *Moody Monthly*, September 1976.

"Candidate Ford and the Catholics," *America*, Sept. 25, 1976.

Casey, Rick, "Carter's Coalition Politics Creates Unease for Catholics," *National Catholic Reporter*, July 30, 1976.

"The Catholic Issues," *Commonweal*, Aug. 27, 1976.

Connell, Anne Stewart, "Who Gets Catholic Vote?" *Des Moines Register*, Aug. 22, 1976.

"Courting the Catholics," *Newsweek*, Sept. 20, 1976.

Evans, Al, "Southern Jews, Baptists and Jimmy Carter," *New York Times*, Oct. 20, 1976.

Friedman, Saul, "Carter Tries to Iron Out His Problems with Catholics," *Philadelphia Inquirer*, July 14, 1976.

Greeley, Andrew M., "Carter and the Catholics," *New York Sunday News*, Aug. 22, 1976.

_____"Carter Needs Catholic Vote," *San Francisco Chronicle*, July 17, 1976.

_____"The Catholic Vote," *New York Sunday News*, Aug. 1, 1976.

_____"Catholics Should Be Fearful of Carter," *Catholic Review*, Aug. 27, 1976.

Greenfield, Meg, "Carter and the Once Born," *Newsweek*, Aug. 2, 1976.

Grieder, William, "Carter's Catholic Problem," *Washington Post*, Aug. 13, 1976.

"Guard Against Christian Political Organizations," *Baptist Standard*, Aug. 4, 1976.

Hart, Jeffrey, "Carter Appeals to Religious Constituency," *Post-Crescent,* May 4, 1976.

Himmelfarb, Milton, "Carter and the Jews," *Commentary,* August 1976.

Hunt, Albert R., "Carter and Catholics," *Wall Street Journal,* July 8, 1976.

Johnson, Haynes, "Catholic Voters Viewed as Problem for Carter," *Washington Post,* July 16, 1976.

Johnston, James M., "Politicians Woo the Evangelical Right," *Milwaukee Sentinel,* May 22, 1976.

Phillips, Kevin P., "Jimmy Carter and the Catholics," *Boston Herald American,* Sept. 22, 1976.

"Politics from the Pulpit," *Newsweek,* Sept. 6, 1976.

Royko, Mike, "The Catholic Vote and Jimmy Carter," *Chicago Daily News,* Aug. 8, 1976.

Squires, Jim, "Carter's Catholic Problem," *Chicago Tribune,* Aug. 9, 1976.

Thimmesch, Nick, "Carter Flirts with Catholics," *Los Angeles Times,* Aug. 30, 1976.

Wallis, Jim, and Michaelson, Wes, "The Plan to Save America: A Disclosure of an Alarming Political Initiative by the Evangelical Far Right," *Sojourners,* Vol. 5, No. 4 (April 1976).

Wills, Garry, "Carter Doesn't Have a Catholic Problem," *Washington Post,* Aug. 21, 1976.

———"Catholics and Evangelicals in Political Equations," *Washington Star,* June 28, 1976.

———"To Seek Catholic Vote: Don't Ask the Bishops," *Washington Star,* Sept. 13, 1976.

Wright, Elliott, "Can Carter Carry the Catholic Vote?" Religious News Service, July 13, 1976.

———"Carter's Evangelical Religion Is Seen as No Issue in Campaign," Religious News Service, July 19, 1976.